R. Richardson

PELICAN BOOKS

CLIMBING IN BRITAIN

(A 160)

PELICAN BOOKS

CLIMBING IN BRITAIN

Edited by

J. E. Q. BARFORD

Honorary Secretary,
The British Mountaineering Council

published by

PENGUIN BOOKS

HARMONDSWORTH MIDDLESEX ENGLAND

245 FIFTH AVENUE NEW YORK U.S.A.

Published in Pelican Books 1946

MADE AND PRINTED IN ENGLAND
FOR PENGUIN BOOKS LTD.
BY ERIC BEMROSE LIMITED LIVERPOOL

CONTENTS

ACKNOWLEDGMENTS

Many climbers have co-operated in the production of this book; but the following should be mentioned in particular as they have provided substantial material: A. T. Hargreaves (Fell and Rock Climbing Club) for elementary climbing, J. H. B. Bell (Scottish Mountaineering Club) for winter climbing, A. S. Pigott (Secretary of the First Aid Committee of Mountaineering Clubs) and Wilson Hey (Chairman of the same body) for the substance of Chapter VIII and Appendix III.

A sub-committee of the Mountaineering Section of the Camping Club of Great Britain contributed the substance of Chapter VII.

The responsibility for any errors remains, however, the editor's alone.

The line illustrations have been contributed by Dr. T. C. L. Parry, to whose patience and ability to draw with cold hands on a Welsh mountain side in winter the editor must pay tribute.

We are further indebted to John Bartholomew & Sons Ltd. for permission to re-publish their glossary of Norse and Gælic place-names: to Major J. H. Emlyn Jones, R.E. (Climbers' Club) for the preparation of the corresponding Welsh glossary; and to Robert Lawrie for the loan of certain illustrations from his Catalogue.

Lastly, but most important, Geoffrey Winthrop Young has played a great part in moulding an engineer's amateurish first attempt at editing into something approaching a book.

J. E. Q. B.

ILLUSTRATIONS

Chapter 1

INTRODUCTION

THIS book is a guide to climbing in Great Britain. While the opportunity is taken occasionally to point out where a principle holds good also for the Alps, or how in the Alps it would be varied, it is not thought necessary to include the actual techniques of Alpine climbing, about which there are many excellent books. About British climbing there are none reasonably up to date, and it is only dealt with in passing in the books about Alpine phases of the sport. The basic principles laid down in such books as Winthrop Young's *Mountain Craft* of course are true of all mountaineering, and any real enthusiast will take the earliest opportunity of reading this book and of benefiting by its precepts and by its analysis of the philosophy of climbing. But here we are going to keep our feet on the ground; we shall not attempt to deal with the theory of the sport; and only with such techniques as are needed for British rock, snow and ice.

Firstly, how has it all come about? In this country the popularity of rock climbing and hill walking has been a comparatively recent phenomenon. In the 19th century there were a certain number of people, mostly drawn from the professional or prosperous classes, who walked for pleasure in the mountainous districts of Britain. During the second half of the same century mountain climbing was discovered as a sport, the credit being largely due to British pioneers from the same groups, who went to the Alps to climb.

As the result of the progress made in this Alpine mountaineering, men began to look for opportunities to practise a part at least of their technique in Britain; and during the 1890's the sport of rock climbing, as such, in this country was born.

About the turn of the century the rock climbers found that they could pursue their sport more readily and sociably if they associated in clubs; and a succession of climbing clubs, mostly local in character, was formed. These clubs formed nurseries for the development of climbing and mountain craft: among their members experience and good traditions were passed on by word of mouth and in their club journals which had, of course, only a very limited circulation.

In the next period, between the two great wars, there was a marked increase in popular interest in hills. This was assisted by the spreading of the Youth Hostels movement; but it was principally due to the growing realisation, by every stratum in our people, that open air activities were a good thing for their own sake.

Unfortunately, most of those who thus began to come to the hills did not know that any clubs existed capable of showing them how to climb or scramble among crags with safety or how to walk over hills with the maximum ease. So it came about that by the end of that period the vast majority of people met with on easy or difficult mountains in Britain belonged to no club, and had no knowledge of the traditions or the techniques of the sport; and, even though most of them were creditably anxious to climb safely, they had little idea where they could look for information and advice.

A contributory factor to this ignorance has been that even when a keen young walker or climber did wish to join a club, often he could not do so, because the clubs demanded a technical qualification before admitting him. He was forced therefore to learn by his own experience, and sometimes to learn dangerously. It was inevitable that a tragic consequence of this unguided development should be a great increase in the number of climbing accidents and of the deaths due to exposure on mountains in winter and summer alike.

Since the beginning of the war further developments have been taking place. In particular, the fighting and national services have been approaching individual climbers and climbing clubs for advice on the techniques and equipment needed for mountain warfare, and to recommend them suitable men to act as instructors in the art of traversing mountain country.

Again, there has been a steadily increasing recognition of the extent to which mountaineering and hill craft can be made to contribute to the healthy education of independent and good citizens, as much as to the more immediate production of sound and self-reliant soldiers. Examples of the new interest are to be found in the launching of the County Badge scheme, and in the character of the training given at such schools as the Outward Bound Sea School at Aberdovey or Gordonstoun School. Educational circles in this country, not a little inspired by Mr. Geoffrey Winthrop Young, have come to see the value of mountain adventure and of the discipline of climbing in developing fortitude, enterprise, endurance and co-operation in the character of adolescent boys.

To meet these changing conditions, the British Mountaineering Council was formed, in 1944. This Council represents the following clubs :

THE ALPINE CLUB
THE ALPINE SKI CLUB
THE ASSOCIATION OF BRITISH MEMBERS OF SWISS ALPINE CLUB
THE BIRMINGHAM UNIVERSITY MOUNTAINEERING CLUB
THE CAIRNGORM CLUB
THE CAMBRIDGE UNIVERSITY MOUNTAINEERING CLUB
THE CLIMBERS' CLUB
THE DERBYSHIRE PENNINE CLUB
THE EDINBURGH UNIVERSITY MOUNTAINEERING CLUB
THE FELL AND ROCK CLIMBING CLUB
THE GRAMPIAN CLUB
THE GRITSTONE CLUB
THE IMPERIAL COLLEGE MOUNTAINEERING CLUB
THE JUNIOR MOUNTAINEERING CLUB OF SCOTLAND
THE LADIES' ALPINE CLUB
THE LIVERPOOL UNIVERSITY MOUNTAINEERING CLUB

THE LOMOND MOUNTAINEERING CLUB
THE MANCHESTER UNIVERSITY MOUNTAINEERING CLUB
THE MIDLAND ASSOCIATION OF MOUNTAINEERS
THE MOUNTAINEERING SECTION OF THE CAMPING CLUB
THE OXFORD UNIVERSITY MOUNTAINEERING CLUB
THE PINNACLE CLUB
THE ROYAL ARTILLERY ALPINE CLUB
THE RUCKSACK CLUB
THE SCOTTISH MOUNTAINEERING CLUB
THE SHEFFIELD UNIVERSITY MOUNTAINEERING CLUB
THE TRICOUNI CLUB
THE WAYFARERS' CLUB
THE YORKSHIRE RAMBLERS' CLUB

As almost its first action, this body decided to issue a book on British mountaineering, for which there is present urgent need, and which it is expected will be increasingly in demand now the war has finished and the energy of our people finds natural outlet in our hill regions again.

The Council therefore empowered me to co-opt any helpers I might need, and to edit a booklet giving the technical information essential to any beginner in British hills, if he is to learn to hill-walk, or to rock-climb safely and efficiently.

In conclusion, I should add that we estimate that at least nine out of ten mountain accidents in Britain are due to ignorance, or carelessness, or both. If this book can reduce the number due to ignorance, it will have achieved the better half of its purpose. If, further, it can make climbing more interesting and easier of performance for those who already know a little about it, it will fulfil all the hopes we have for it.

Chapter 2

CHOICE OF COMPANION, EQUIPMENT AND FOOD

IF you have not walked or climbed on hills before, there are a few general points you should have in mind before you start.

Companion

You may prefer to go alone, and certainly some of the finest of memories are of hours passed walking alone among hills. But, until you have some experience, it is folly to walk alone upon unknown hills except in settled fair weather. A mist, or a storm, or a blinding wind, and the best of us may go astray, and be out for a night of anxiety to other people. Or a twisted ankle may risk your life by long exposure, and can always involve much and long distress for those who have to search for you.

For hill walking, the pleasantest company is someone of your own age with whom you can share the responsibilities and adventures equally. But be sure he is a stout fellow; because rough weather and rough going and fatigue try tempers furiously, and a very agreeable every-day friend may crack up badly under what is bound at its best to be a pretty tough test of endurance and comradeship. When, however, you are once started on the mountain adventure together, remember that you are bound to see it through together; and that the more the one of you proves to be the weaker physically, or the less good-humoured under hardship, the more the other is bound to stay with him and to see him safely through, at least as far as to an agreed parting in some safe centre.

No one should ever rock-climb alone, even upon a chance-met crag, until he is an experienced rock climber and knows exactly his own ability and how to make the right allowance for the additional dangers of solitary climbing—which are many.

For rock climbing it is always better at the start to have at least one in the party who knows what he is about on rocks, and can advise you in the elementary technique. Good climbers, of course, are always ready to help, and on British cliffs, if it is the kind of weather in which novices ought to be climbing rocks at all, there is usually a good chance of meeting someone who can give advice, or even spare an hour or so for a little practical instruction. But it is much better to arrange beforehand to have some practical guidance at the start from a climber, even if it is only for a day or two of your hill holiday.

If you can't get an introduction to a climber, even through a friend, try writing to the secretary of the nearest local climbing club and see if he can help; or find out if the Youth Hostels Association, or the Council for Physical Recreation have a climbing section or meet in your district. You may count on it that climbers everywhere are always ready to help a keen beginner.

Never forget that mountains which look, and indeed are, so friendly and straightforward in sunny weather, can become very suddenly dangerous, if anything at all goes wrong either with the weather, or your companion, or yourself.

Once you have arranged your party you can discuss together all the absorbing details of your equipment.

Equipment and Food

As we hope that this book will still be current when full peace returns it assumes peace conditions both among the mountains and in our shopping. A minimum equipment is essential both for hill walking and for climbing; luckily for us the minimum is pretty simple and inexpensive, and it is partly this lack of expense which has made climbing and hill walking popular.

Clothing for Hill Walking in Summer

Your first care should be a pair of strong, well nailed and well-fitting boots. Shoes although lighter are not satisfactory as they do not give the protection required by your ankles in rough walking. Boots will prevent your ankle being bruised and a violent wrench is less likely to produce a strained or sprained ankle.

Most people prefer to have boots large enough to allow of two pairs of thick socks or stockings inside them both for comfort in walking and warmth in winter.

The tongues of the boots should be sewn in at the sides, so that the boot is waterproof right up to the ankles.

The best method of nailing boots for hill walking and climbing is still a subject of controversy among climbers and is dealt with later in the climbing equipment section. For hill walking a comparatively simple nailing using clinkers and mugger hobs only is probably the most satisfactory (such as 1, 2 and 6 of Fig. 2). Tricounis (as in illustration, Fig. 4) although used for rock climbing are definitely not too satisfactory for British hill walking. Clinker nails round the edges are cheaper, will last longer and will not trip the walker up when boulder hopping. For those who cannot afford to buy a proper pair of climbing boots with clinker or tricouni nailing, quite an adequate arrangement for hill walking is to have hobs put in any suitable boot

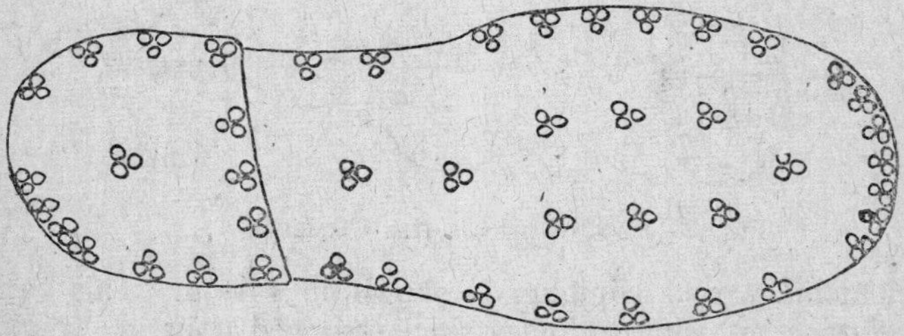

FIG. 1—A SIMPLE FORM OF BOOTNAILING FOR HILL WALKING

by a competent cobbler. Standard army boots are most satisfactory when nailed. An arrangement which has proved satisfactory in service both for hill walking and for

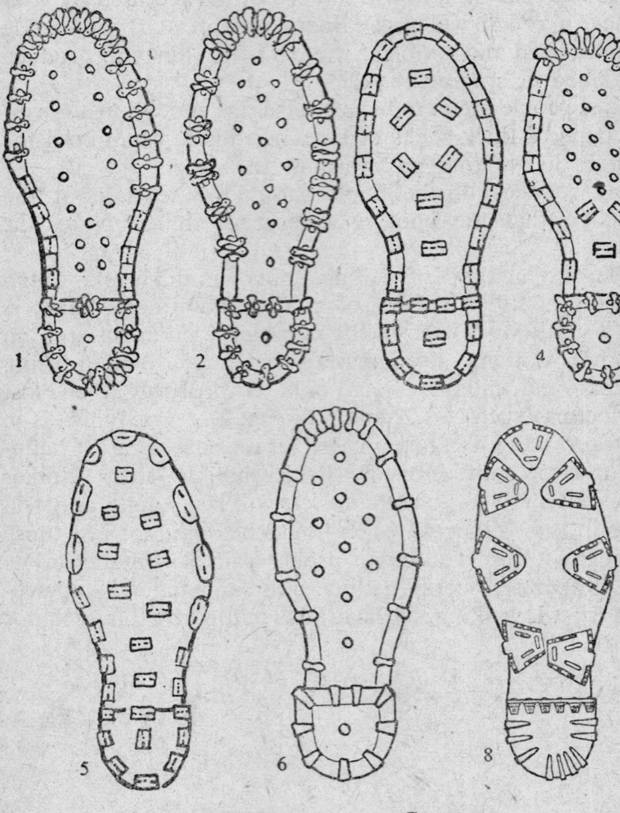

FIG. 2—BOOT NAILINGS FOR CLIMBERS

elementary rock-climbing is shown in Fig. 1. This can be done by using ordinary single-pronged hobs in groups of three, or " three-in-one " hobs singly.

One point about clothing has already been mentioned, the desirability of wearing two pairs of socks for long or rough walking. These should be thick and woollen, a pair of stockings underneath with a pair of socks over them folded down over the boot-tops to keep out small scree. Puttees can be used for the same purpose. The chief point about the rest of the clothing is that it should be warm enough and allow free movement of the body and the limbs. Within these limits you may choose as you please, and it is not proposed to make detailed suggestions here. However it is important to remember when dressing for the day that it will be much colder on the hills than at your starting point in the valley. Even in summer the conditions on our native hills can quickly become arctic, and spare sweaters and windproof clothing should always be carried. Cold and especially cold wind or cold rain can rapidly lower your vitality and ability to walk or climb and you should always guard against its dangers. On the other hand no satisfactory precaution can be taken against the perennial rain which falls upon our islands. Whatever combination of capes, sou'-westers and leggings you wear it is virtually impossible to keep dry in heavy rain, and climbers and walkers must grow resigned to getting soaked to the skin on a really wet day. Some of the windproof cloths on the market will withstand light rain or a short shower, and it is possible to delay the soak by wearing such clothing on top.

A hat with a stout brim is useful to stop the rain trickling down your neck; some prefer to have some sort of chin-strap to hold it in position.

Trousers or shorts are another matter of controversy. Shorts give the greater freedom, the better ventilation and are less unpleasant when wet, but in cold or wintry weather the wearer will get thoroughly chilled long before the wearer of trousers. In fact in view of the number of deaths from exposure in winter on our hills, many due to this cause, it should be emphasized that shorts should never be worn in winter except in a period of settled and windless weather.

There is also slight disagreement on the best method of supporting the trousers: braces are perhaps to be preferred as allowing greater freedom of movement; belts on most figures have to be worn too tight and constrict the organs if they are to remain secure during violent movement or when clothes are wet.

Clothing for Hill Walking in Winter

In winter more spare sweaters should be carried; thick gloves, probably best of wool, should be worn. A woollen scarf and a balaclava helmet are useful extra items.

Other Equipment for Hill Walking

An indispensable item is a good map of the district, either a 1″ Ordnance Survey or a Bartholomew's large scale district map. The Ordnance Survey is slightly better because it is more detailed and the contour lines are at a less interval—an important help when traversing hill country. A compass must always be taken to enable intelligent use to be made of the map in mist or at night. The standard army pattern prismatic, particularly of the liquid-filled type, is probably the best, but cheaper ones of simpler construction meet most needs.

If there is any likelihood of your not being back before dark you should carry an electric torch or lantern. Even if you do not need it to pick the way across rough country it will still be needed to read the map.

Each party if not each man will require a rucksack to carry the lunch and spare clothing. A frame rucksack while it feels more comfortable is not really best for the purpose: it is bulky, and since the centre of gravity of the load is farther back than with a frameless type, your balance in walking or climbing is not so secure or stable. It is better to have a rucksack with no pockets than a smaller one with large projecting awkward ones.

For really heavy loads, such as may have to be carried by camping parties in winter, pack frames of the Yukon (Plate 1), Greene or Packer Nelson type are preferable because up to 70 lb. may be carried fairly comfortably. These frames and the full size Bergen are, however, only suitable to carry the size of load you need for a complete holiday or camping expedition. A small light frameless

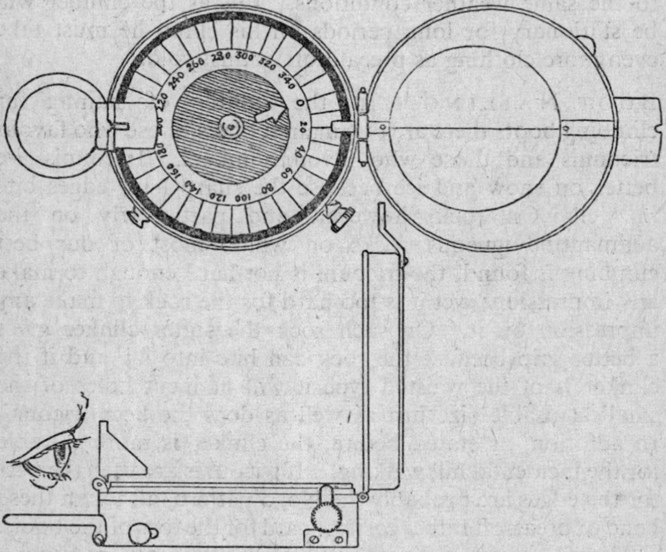

FIG. 3—THE PRISMATIC COMPASS

rucksack is enough for a day's expedition and should be taken. Each member of your party should carry a box of matches and a sharp knife.

A simple first aid kit is indispensable. This should contain as a minimum some Elastoplast and an iodine pen. A further outfit can be carried with advantage; particularly useful are an elastic bandage and a pair of scissors.

A light ice-axe should be carried in winter. This is dealt with in the climbing section of this chapter.

Equipment for Climbing

All the equipment detailed for hill-walking is required also for climbing, because the climber has to do a certain amount of hill walking to get to and from his cliff and he is exposed to the same weather conditions. But as the climber will be stationary for long periods on his climb he must take even more clothing as precaution against cold.

BOOT NAILING. In the matter of nailing for climbing boots there are two main schools, those who favour tricounis and those who favour clinkers. Tricounis are better on snow and ice because the sharp hard edges bite in well. On rock, however, and particularly on the adamantine igneous rocks on which most of our best climbing is found, the tricouni is not hard enough to make any impression; yet it is too hard for the rock to make any impression on it. On such rock the softer clinker gives a better grip because the rock can bite into it; and if the clinker is of the waisted type it will fit incut holes of the smallest usable size just as well as does the keen tricouni. In addition, as stated before, the clinker is more suitable for the incidental hill walking. If tricounis are used the best for the edges are probably the No. 5 pattern, although these bend or break off rather easily if used for the toes of the boots.

The fit of your boots for climbing is all important. While for walking it is desirable to have boots big enough for two pairs of stockings, for climbing it is more important to have the sole of your boot correspond as nearly as possible with the sole of your foot, especially for delicate or open climbing, because this avoids excessive leverage on the ankles. You must keep this compromise in mind in choosing your boots. One well-known climber, fortunately with small feet, uses two separate pairs of boots, one for walking and the other for climbing.

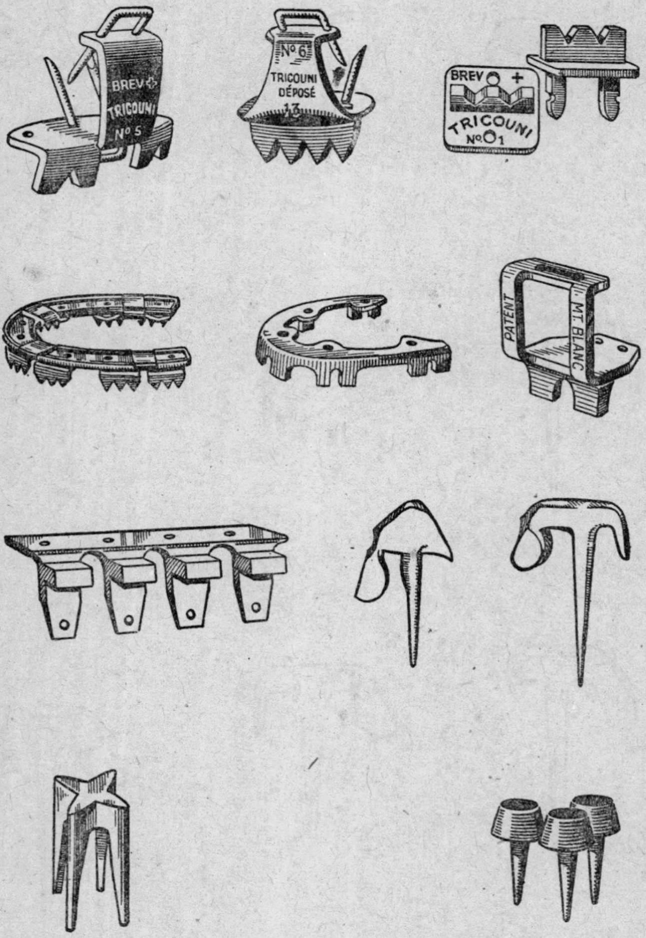

FIG. 4—SOME CLIMBING NAILS

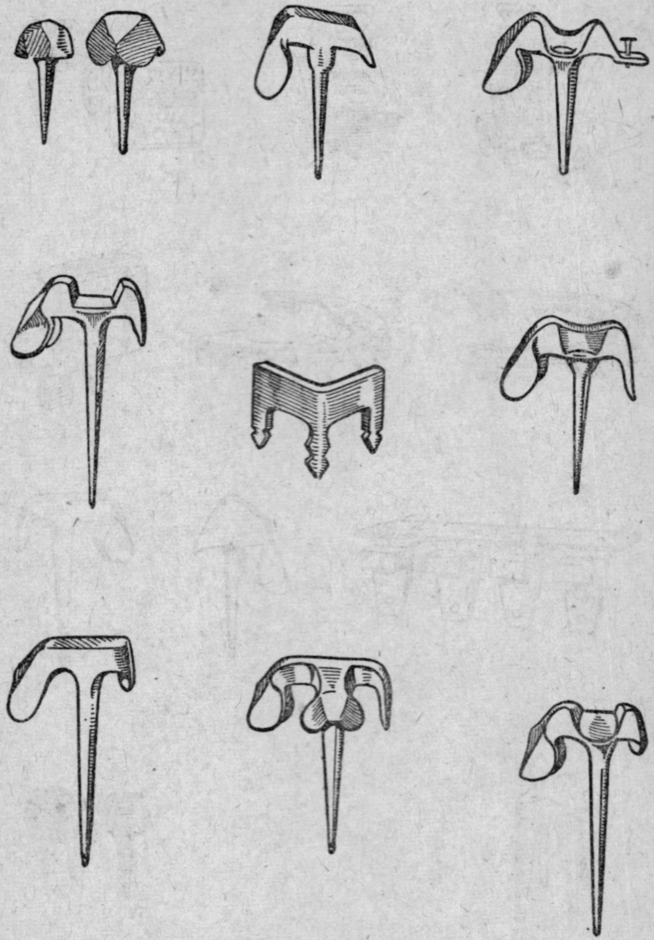

FIG. 5—MORE CLIMBING NAILS

ROPE AND LINE. Nothing in the rock-climber's equipment calls for more attention than the rope. The rope is in a sense his insurance policy and no care or expense is too great to lavish on its choice and use. Until the outbreak of the war the best ropes were considered to be of manila hemp, Italian hemp or flax. But experience in the services has shown the virtue of nylon and it is not improbable that soon this may become the standard rope. Meanwhile, I shall say nothing further here as to the respective merits.

There are three main weights of rope in general use, known colloquially as "rope," as "three-quarter" and as "line." For one well-known type of cordage the comparative figures are as follows:—

	Wt. per 100 ft.	*Diameter in mm.*	*Ultimate strength*
Rope ...	5 lb. 12 oz.	11	1.6 tons
¾	4 lb. 6 oz.	10	1.2 tons
Line ...	2 lb. 12 oz.	8	17 cwt.

These figures apply actually to a rope from manila hemp, but they apply approximately to all good climbing ropes, except nylon. The percentage extension of the rope at its ultimate load is as important as its ultimate strength, because it is the amount of energy which a rope will absorb in an emergency which determines whether or not it will break. For those interested, references to technical articles on the strength of climbing ropes are given in the bibliography (Chapter 11).

It cannot be too strongly emphasized that beginners should always climb on a full weight rope. If parties of experts are found to climb on line or on ¾ weight, it is because the weight of the line hanging from the leader's waist high up on a long pitch such as they habitually climb, is not such a hindrance to them as would be the heavier, if safer, rope. The drag of a full weight rope on a 100 foot runout on vertical or near-vertical rocks has to be felt to be believed, especially if the rope happens also to be wet. But novices have first to learn how to climb safely; and for secure climbing the full weight rope must be used. As you advance in expertness $\frac{3}{4}$ weight is a compromise you may reasonably adopt. A length of 120 ft. of this rope for two climbers is a satisfactory safeguard for practically all Welsh and English rock climbs, provided that the users are experienced and continue to allow for its lower strength.

Special care must also be given to the storage and use of the rope. It should be dried carefully after use, but not in front of a fire. It should never be stretched when wet. It should be stored in a cool dry place, and not in one used also for the storage of any liquid or solid likely to give off noxious or corrosive vapours. In using it you should make certain that the rope is not dragged over, or belayed round, sharp-edged rocks which will fray it, and that you do not tread on it in nailed boots. No rope which has once been over-strained by a fall should ever be used again as it will be most seriously weakened; nor any rope which has been badly bruised or cut. As a measure of economy it is permissible to cut out an injured section of the rope and splice the join, but you should recognize that it will then be considerably weaker and the splice will give trouble in recovering the rope after a rope-down.

SLINGS. Most parties doing exposed or difficult rock climbs nowadays carry one or more slings. These consist of lengths of from 5 ft. to 7 ft. of rope or line which can be joined at the ends by a reef (Fig. 6) or fisherman's knot (Fig. 7), so as to make loops of any size required at the moment, and they are used for many kinds of belays and in emergency for roping down. A leader may well carry two or three; and one at least should be of line, since this can be used for belaying in many places on cliffs where a rope sling would not go.

The method of application of slings is described later. Some people have the slings already spliced up so as to form continuous loops. But this is not recommended, because it makes them less adjustable. Also it is important that the slings be made of good rope or line, because when used as belays they may have to take the greatest strain. On no account use old rope for this purpose.

FIG. 6—THE REEF KNOT

FIG. 7—THE FISHERMAN'S KNOT

PITONS. The English word is pegs; but the French word has been in currency for some years and may be retained for the present. Pitons are pegs or large nails with rings in one end, which are driven into rocks to provide an anchor where no natural one exists, or to assist the climber, mechanically, to get up. The latter usage is common in some continental ranges but is considered bad form in this country.

They are made in a large variety of shapes as shown in Fig. 8. Pitons of thin leaf alloy steel have been found the most serviceable in this country. A leader may well carry two of these aids.

SNAPLINKS. These are called karabiners in Germany and mousquetons in France, and consist of an oval steel ring with a spring-loaded hinged link in one side, rather like an enlarged version of the clip on the end of a watch-chain. The name "spring-eyes" or "spring-clips" would probably describe them more correctly. They are useful devices for making running belays or for attaching a sling to the waist loop on a fixed belay. The latter usage allows of a quick and neat transfer of the belay from leader to second, and from second to last man, as the

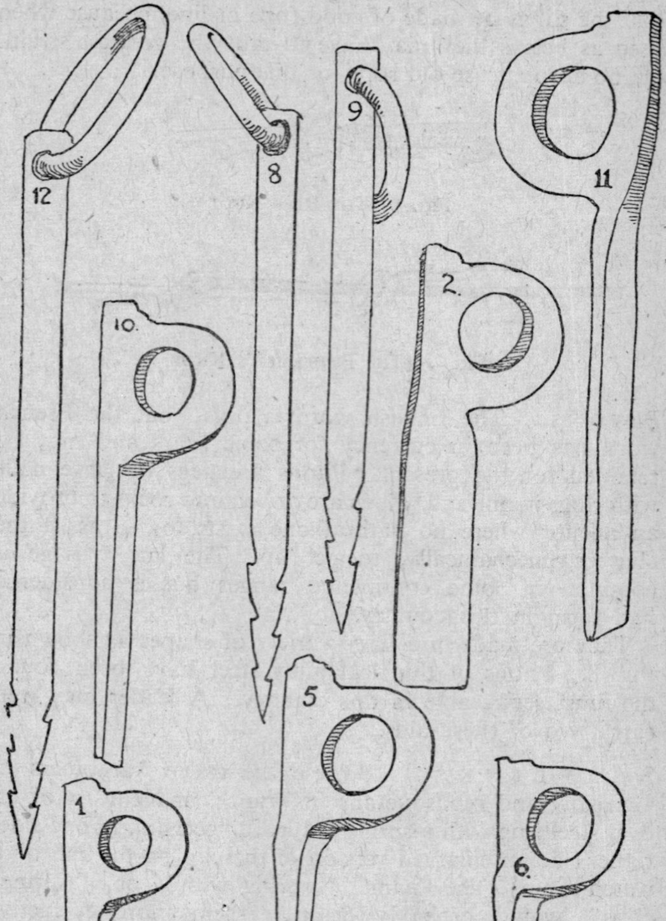

FIG. 8—PEGS

party moves up the cliff, the same sling being used and merely transferred from one waist loop to the next as the climbers ascend.

RUBBERS. The simple rock climber as opposed to the all-round mountaineer usually carries and wears rubber shoes—" sneakers " as the Americans graphically call them—for hard rock climbing in dry weather. These are admirable on dry but virtually useless on wet, muddy or iced rock. The occasions on which they can be used in this country are therefore limited, although on those occasions they make rock climbing much easier except on limestone where felt is still better and confer a new delight in the feeling of freedom and lightness which they give to the wearer. Owing to their many limitations it is essential that the beginner should first learn to climb competently in boots. If the reverse course is followed a rapid change in the weather may at any time confront him with some comparatively simple problem which he is quite incapable of solving. On dry rock rubbers give greatly improved friction and it is possible to adhere with the rubber-shod foot in many places which provide no hold for boots. Their proper place is on dry slab and crack climbing. But on steep walls where there are only small square incut holes, such as the East Wall of Idwal Slabs, in North Wales, boots will be as good or better.

Rubbers, of course, wear away the rocks less and it has been suggested that certain climbs which are both good and popular should be closed to the nail-shod climber so as to ensure that they will remain for posterity. So far no great notice has been taken of this suggestion, although one hears that the wearing of boots on the Pinnacle Face of Scafell is frowned upon, also at Helsby and on the soft sandstone cliffs near Tunbridge Wells which are the only resort of the London climber, because the use of boots would very rapidly remove some of the best climbs from the faces of these cliffs.

If you wish to wear rubbers you should buy them to fit you when you are wearing only one pair of stockings or socks. The best have thin black rubber soles, like the cheapest variety of " gym " shoe that could be bought before the war. Crêpe is bad as it is more adversely affected by damp than cheap black rubber. The shoe should be flexible so that the foot and toes can be flexed almost as well as if they were bare. Before the war one boot and shoe chain store sold a boot with a thick rubber sole with canvas uppers which extended above the ankle and with rubber guards to protect the ankle bones. These were excellent, and a boot retains its shape longer than a shoe.

KLETTERSCHUHE. These are another form of footwear evolved to suit the dolomite rock of Tyrol. They are boots with felt soles and soft leather uppers. Similar boots with rope or string soles are called scarpetti in Italy and espadrilles in France. All this kind of footwear gives almost as great friction on dry rock as does rubber and has the advatage that it does not lose its grip on wet rock. But even such footwear becomes quite hopeless in the muddy places which you will find on British cliffs.

SOCKS. If conditions are unsuitable for rubbers or no rubbers are available a section of a climb which is too difficult for boots may be climbed in socks. These give as good friction on wet rock as kletterschuhe (until they wear out) and provide a most desirable freedom for the toes.

Additional Equipment for Climbing in Winter

GLOVES. The right gloves for climbing remain a problem. Climbers use many varieties and this variety itself shows that there is no completely satisfactory solution. If you intend to climb rock it is essential that you should have your fingers free; and consequently many climbers use fingerless mittens which keep the wrists and back of the hands warm, while leaving the fingers free. To guard against the fingers going numb in very cold weather climbers often carry overgloves of Grenfell cloth or leather which they can put on over the mittens in the intervals between climbing pitches. This is probably the best solution yet found.

An alternative is to wear cotton gloves of the normal type. These can be worn while climbing and if a reasonable good fit they will give you freedom and a good grip on all except the smallest holds.

ICE-AXE. In winter if there is much snow about an ice-axe is essential unless the climbing is to be confined to the small cliffs below the snowline. It is equally necessary for a winter walking expedition if the party intends to go over the tops because a high ridge or a slope which may be an easy scramble in summer may become in winter a formidable problem of the Alpine type.

Climbers have as many opinions about ice-axes as fly fishermen about flies. The dimensions given below for a good axe are a compromise between what is most convenient in ascent in the constricted space of a gully, and what is most convenient in step cutting downwards or for glissading :—

Length of haft—head to end of spike 34″—36″
Length of pick—7″
Length of adze—4½″

The haft should be oval so that it does not slide round in your grip. It should be made of straight grained hickory or ash. The pick should be straight on the underside, and the whole of the head made of medium tempered mild steel. Some manufacturers put saw tooth notches in the underside of the pick, which are neither useful nor harmful. There should be no collar on the haft to prevent the sling coming off, and the spike and ferrule should be fixed quite separately. A combined spike and ferrule is weak and does not allow the desirable amount of give when a sudden strain is put on it.

Many British climbers who do not need to use the axe for sounding snow bridges over crevasses, put in a brass or phosphor bronze screw on one side of the haft to prevent the sling coming off. In climbs which are a mixture of snow and rock, this screw is a great convenience but it may weaken the haft a little. The sling should be of stout woven material attached to a steel ring which is big enough to slide freely along the haft but not to pass over the stop-screw.

THE SMALL EXTRA ICE-AXE. This may be of use to a leader on difficult ice-pitches to use as an additional hold and to save borrowing another man's axe. It can

FIG. 9—THE HORESCHOWSKY PITON HAMMER

well be an adapted slater's hammer with the shaft cut down and the hammer end shortened to about 2″ long. Its use may obviate unsafe combined tactics. Some climbers use a more finished article—the Horeschowsky piton hammer; this while primarily intended as a piton hammer has a pick as well as a hammer head and a short haft. In the confined gullies of Wales, the Lakes and Scotland which provide the best and hardest winter climbing, it is often useful.

CRAMPONS OR CLAWS. These are unnecessary on British mountains. They encourage a slovenly technique and they may lead an incompetent party into an impossible situation from which they can neither advance nor retreat.

ICE PITONS. Ice pitons of foreign manufacture are illustrated with the rock pitons. 9″ to 15″ lengths of steel tube, buffed at one end, are equally serviceable.

Equipment for Camping

CLOTHING. The clothing required is the same as for hill walking, but a complete spare change should always be taken, and kept in the tent in wet weather. The temptation to put on your spare change on the second wet or doubtful day instead of the clothes wetted the day before should be resisted. To return to camp and to have no dry change at all to get into is a miserable business and entails retiring to your sleeping bag.

TENTS. The tent is vastly important. A climber's whole enjoyment may be spoilt by anxiety as to the stability of his tent during daylight when he is away or at night when he should be asleep. Unfortunately, no really suitable stock tent which will stand up to the severe weather—wind and rain—experienced in British mountains is at present on the market. Most tent-makers will of course make one to your own design to order. The stock model nearest to the ideal is probably the "Arctic Guinea."

Since we assume that solitary climbing is unwise, the two-man tent is taken as a basis, so that we avoid the difficulty of trying to combine robustness and lightness in a one-man tent. In this way comfort for two may be attained and perhaps three may be sheltered. Reasonable economy in weight is possible for a party equipped with such a tent as the load of the common equipment can be shared.

The tent should preferably be of the "A" form (see

illustration) to provide the maximum useful space and stability possible for the given dimensions under conditions of wind and rain. One-pole tents are hardly suitable, especially one-guy tents which depend on finding even ground for a good set. Willesden proofed canvas is the best material for the tent. Very light materials are not strong enough to last and do not withstand driving rain.

The groundsheet should be sewn into the tent and the

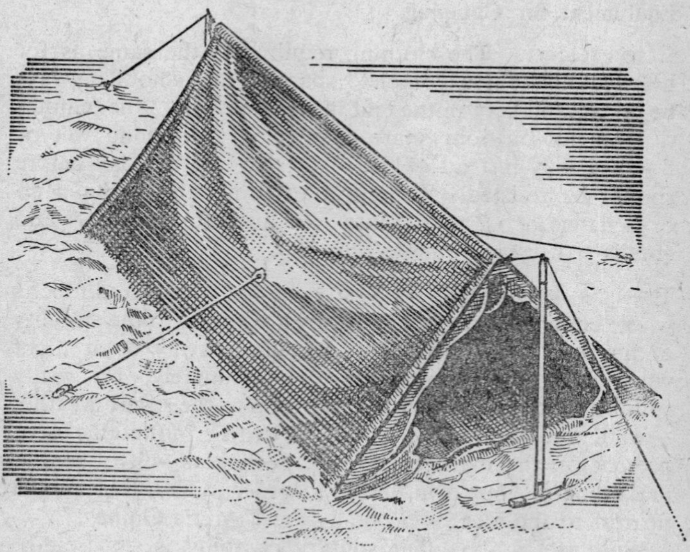

FIG. 10—A MOUNTAIN TENT

resulting shortened life must be accepted. A wear of at least two seasons may be counted upon. Rubberised fabric is to be avoided but most of the oiled or painted lightweight fabrics sold for the purpose are excellent.

The poles should either be one of the " A " type and one straight, or preferably, to increase the stability, both of the

" A " type. They should be light-weight—of jointed dural tube or of bamboo. The " A " joint must be made sound mechanically. The tent should sit by grummetts on a collar directly on to the poles or " A " joints. The customary $\frac{1}{4}''$ diameter spike of standard tents is not strong enough. The pole sections should not exceed 15″ in length.

An outside valance should be provided all round the tent to be weighted by rocks or snow for greater security. Pegs alone are inadequate.

The ordinary lace-up doors provide better ventilation and access in good weather; but sleeve doors better withstand prolonged driving rain or snow and incidentally exclude midges.

The guys should be plentiful and strong to stand up to fraying in rough weather when boulders have to be loaded on to the pegs. Provision should be made for stormset guying.

A low wall to the tent, vertical or sloping inwards to the ground and surmounted by a small eave which enables the pull of the guys to be taken in line with the roof of the tent, is necessary.

A flysheet is desirable in heavy rain but none have so far been designed which will stand up to a strong wind. Until the design is improved so as to be reliable, it is not advisable to keep one erected in a high wind. Many will prefer to dispense with this weighty addition and put up with some increased discomfort in wet weather.

The tent ridge should be roped and all seams and points of tension taped.

A bell end to the tent provides extra space for storage of kit with a relatively small increase in weight.

In conclusion it must be stressed that camping in mountains is a totally different thing to camping as ordinarily practised in this country. In the mountains the ordinary light-weight equipment is useless and all gear will have to stand up to incredibly hard conditions.

BEDDING. A ground blanket of thin cashmere wool or a light weight three-quarter length air-bed is recommended. The sleeping bag should be best eiderdown; goosedown is a less satisfactory alternative. The "Icelandic" bag is outstanding in its class. In very cold weather two sleeping bags can be used. A pillow can be incorporated in the airbed or made from spare clothes.

The practice of sleeping in your outdoor clothes is not to be recommended—unless weather conditions are so bad as to make a midnight flit likely!

STOVES AND COOKING UTENSILS. For efficiency and safety the one pint or half-pint paraffin Primus stoves are undoubtedly the best; but petrol or methylated spirit stoves may be used. A spare jet, a complete set of washers and several prickers should always be carried. Since cooking inside the tent is usually necessary, attention must be paid to its ventilation as these stoves do on occasions generate carbon monoxide. The stove container should be a handleless aluminium saucepan in which the stove is packed with clean rags; they will probably be useful.

FUEL. The fuel is best carried in aluminium hot water bottles or in quart oil tins and a small funnel taken for refilling the stove. The meagre store of paraffin that one can carry permits no wastage.

CANTEENS. For cooking, any of the lightweight nests of canteens are good; a large size should be chosen. A robust "gripit" should be substituted for the patent collapsible handles.

CUPS, PLATES, ETC. Plastic cups and, if needed, plates are best. Take an ordinary knife, fork and spoon; patent ones are unsatisfactory. A tin-opener must not be forgotten; the patent revolving type is small, light, and opens tins neatly, so as to form additional receptacles until camp is struck. A wide-mouthed milkcan which can be closed tightly is useful. The water-bucket weighing one ounce and holding a gallon, made by Benjamin Edginton Ltd. is unapproachable for lightness and will last at least three seasons.

Winter Camping

Winter camping in British hills is even more specialized than summer mountain camping, and all equipment has to be designed for arctic conditions. Since only a very small minority practise it, we will not devote space to it here.

Food

This involves separate questions: what food to take for a party going on a day's climbing and what food to provide for a camping expedition or a climbing holiday or a week-end in a climbing hut or in a Scottish Youth Hostel where usually no meals are provided.

FOOD FOR A DAY'S CLIMBING OR WALKING. Most people keep the food they take out for the day as simple as possible. Chocolate, sardines and dried fruits are ideal; they are compact and sustaining. In our hills you need not carry drink as there is good water in the mountain streams, but fresh fruit is a pleasant variation and a thirst quencher. On certain expeditions such as the traverse of the main ridge of the Cuillin of Skye you may have to carry drink to avoid descending from the ridge to find water. During the present shortage of chocolate and dried fruit most people take sandwiches and cheese if they can get it.

FOOD FOR CAMPING OR LIVING IN HUTS. Food for unprovisioned huts is the same as food for camping, except that for camping you may have to carry it further on the back and so shun all avoidable weight. The main requirements are:—

1. To be light and easy to carry and store. For this dried and dehydrated foods are best.
2. To be easy to cook. Boiling and frying make up

camp cooking but in some of the better equipped huts you can roast, grill and bake as well.

The weight of food taken can be calculated as approximately 2 lb. per head per day, although 2½ to 3 is more usual.

The safest rule to follow is to take as far as possible the things you like. Under cold conditions more sugar and fat are necessary than in a normal diet. Canned foods are very heavy but meat if taken is better canned; dried meat and pemmican are not recommended. Bread and potatoes are heavy and bulky but some campers consider them indispensable. Milk is best taken as dried full-cream powder; but in most places in these islands fresh milk can be obtained (in peace time) from the farms. Cheese is an excellent food and dried eggs can be served at almost any time. Cereals such as oatmeal, macaroni, lentils and so on are a good standby, as are also dried soups. A little onion and carrot help to flavour the evening stew immensely. Plenty of jam is very useful for the sweet course.

Many of these foods are best packed and kept in small linen bags—old flour bags serve quite well.

A representative list of food which will be required is given below:—

ESSENTIAL FOODS

Porridge oats (quick cooking brands) or oatmeal, macaroni, etc.
Biscuits.
Meat extracts.
Dried milk (full cream).
Sugar, sweets, jam.
Butter, cheese and cooking fat.
Nuts.
Tea, coffee, cocoa, Ovaltine, Horlick's malted milk.
Canned meat and fish.
Dried soups.
Dried eggs.
Chocolate.
Dried fruits, e.g., apricots, figs, prunes, dates, raisins.
Salt and pepper.

LUXURIES.

Canned fruit.
Fresh meat.
Bread and cake.
Fresh fruit and vegetables.
Potatoes.
Nuts.

Chapter 3

HILL WALKING

Introduction

THIS section deals with hill walking in Britain in summer and winter but excludes snow conditions which are dealt with separately. Of course it is not necessary, even at the start, to plan and carry out a walk with the care I give to it here: you can just tramp ahead through hills in fine weather and get plenty of fun. But you will feel an altogether finer and freer pleasure if you do the same thing after learning something about hill craft, when you know the meaning of what you see, and can form a fair idea about what you can't see, but which is coming beyond the range and when you know you can rely on yourself to get safely out of any difficulty that a change of weather or an unexpected accident may always produce among mountains. Anyone who takes the trouble to give himself a thorough grounding in reading country and in reading the map will soon be able to keep the rules in mind without bothering about them; then he is a freeman of the hills in the happiest sense.

PLANNING THE ROUTE. The day before the expedition you should work out the route which you intend to follow on the map, taking into account the wishes and capabilities of the rest of the party, the condition of the weather and of the hills. For this purpose I am assuming that you will use a 1″ Ordnance Survey map, although a large scale Bartholomew's is almost equally useful. The 1″ O.S. map is accurate and adequately detailed; on it the contours (the orange lines joining places of equal height above sea-level) are at 50 feet intervals. That is to say, that if you move over the ground from any point on one contour line to any point on the next, you will have climbed or descended 50 feet in vertical height. From this it follows that if the contour lines on the map are close together the hillside will be very steep, if far apart the gradient will be gentle.

Rocky hillsides and cliffs are indicated by shading.

With practice you can make a mental picture of the country from the contours and other conventional signs as they appear on the map. As a beginning it is enough to know that where the contours are bunched closely together the ground will be steep and difficult going.

Try then to trace out the easiest route and to memorise prominent features on it. A rough sketch will help to fix the main features in your memory.

Note the position of difficulties, particularly cliffs and stretches of unbridged rivers, so that you can avoid them when on the ground. Note their general direction so that if you meet them in mist or at night you will know the best way round the cliff or the right direction to find a bridge across the river.

Choose the route so as not to lose height which you will have to regain later. But if to keep height means crossing very rough ground then it is always better to descend. In hills the shortest route between two points is seldom the quickest or easiest.

You can always descend a hillside direct provided it is not craggy or precipitous. Choose the line of descent so that when you get down to the river in the valley you can cross it by a bridge or ford it without a big diversion.

In valleys do not assume that an arbitrary line plotted beforehand on a map can be followed. Landowners, farmers, or even gardeners may obstruct passage and you can avoid unpleasantness and delay by keeping to lanes and footpaths. Dry stone walls are very easily damaged and take long to rebuild: gates in the end give the quicker line.

Good routes seldom follow streams. Water always tries to find the shortest way to the valley and consequently makes for the steepest places. You can usually find a better route along the shoulders of the mountains enclosing the streams.

LENGTH OF ROUTE. Decide how many hours of daylight are available and grade the length of the expedition

FIG. 11—GOOD ROUTES SELDOM FOLLOW STREAMS

accordingly. Aim to be on easy ground or in the valley before nightfall unless you are carrying camping or bivouac equipment.

Measure the overall length carefully, and estimate the amount of uphill going or steep climbing involved. On a flat map, showing hilly country, distances have a misleading look. A precalculation will often prevent a youthful and ambitious party being disappointed when it finds it cannot fulfil its plan for the day or can only do so too tired to enjoy it.

You can estimate length by the following rules:—

Allow one hour for every $2\frac{1}{2}$ miles as measured on the map, and an additional hour for every 1,500 feet climbed.

Particularly rough going, mist, snow or high winds will reduce this speed considerably, and before using this formula for planning a long expedition you should check that it corresponds to your natural pace, or modify it accordingly.

You must allow extra time for halts; and you should always keep some time in hand to allow for mistakes, for emergencies and the small delays that add up to such a lot in a long day.

Remember that the larger the party the more time must be allowed for every section of the day and for every halt. However prompt they may be, time melts away quite unaccountably between the movements of any party of more than three.

Plan never to do as much on the first day as you will expect to be doing later. Hill air and the high spirits of starting a holiday will always encourage you to overdo it at first; and you will pay for it on the second, and all subsequent days.

THE PARTY AND THE LEADER. It is a good thing to know something about each other's capabilities—and weaknesses!—beforehand. On an energetic tour, all should have agreed before starting on the general route, and upon their procedure should anything go wrong with any one of them or with their plans. It should be known which of the party can use map and compass, which of them have climbed or walked among mountains before, and how much they can be counted upon to lead or help the others.

When this is clear, some of the leader's duties as I set them out here can well be divided up.

In an inexperienced party it is found very useful to choose a "leader," the least inexperienced or the most trusted. It falls to him to make the decisions when there is doubt, or in an emergency, and he saves much time in settling small details, or when the party gets tired and cross and wants to argue with each other all round.

Like most leadership, it is more of a burden than an honour; for although it is part of his duties to divide up the jobs and assign them among the others, it always still lies with him to see that those jobs are done properly and up to time; and, however tired and wet himself, he has always to be able to bring out just that extra reserve of strength and good humour that will keep up the tone of the party under depressing conditions.

As experience of hills and knowledge of each other grows, the need for a recognized "leader" diminishes: until a party finds it is acting altogether in harmony and by common agreement, and that every detail is being seen to without any call for a leader or his reminders.

THE FINAL CHECK. Immediately before starting the leader must check to his own satisfaction that the party has all the necessary equipment: map, compass, lamp, whistle, money and sufficient food.

Every member of the party should know who is carrying that part of the equipment they will all be using and who has the spare compasses, maps and lanterns if there are any.

The leader must see also that the compass and the lantern work properly; that all are properly clothed and have some spare clothing with them; in particular that their footwear is satisfactory and has been tried out beforehand. He should check that all know the agreed signals, with whistles, or calls or lights.

The Expedition

ROUTE FINDING IN CLEAR WEATHER. In clear weather direction can be maintained by direct map reading and landmarks better than by compass bearings.

If the whole of the route can be seen from the starting point choose the easiest cross country line and memorise landmarks on it—houses, curiously shaped rocks, streams, sheepfolds and so on. When you are under weigh you may no longer be able to see the further route or its objective; the intermediate marks which have been memorized will then enable the party to keep on the right line.

When going up a hillside from a valley or a flat plain you will be able to see behind you a road, a river, a railway, the edge of a field or a wood, and you can use this as a pointer by which you can continue to keep direction, even when both your remote objective ahead and the intermediate landmarks you have noted are blotted out by a fold in the ground, a wood or a wall.

Therefore, make a habit of looking back occasionally. In difficult country, supposing bad weather or darkness make it advisable to turn back, a memory of what the country looked like when seen in the reverse direction may prove most valuable.

In daytime the position of the sun will give you approximate directions as follows :—

BRITISH SUMMER TIME

At 7 a.m.	the sun	is	East
At 10 a.m.	„	„	South-East
At 1 p.m.	„	„	South
At 4 p.m.	„	„	South-West
At 7 p.m.	„	„	West

In double summer time reckon an hour later for each position of the sun.

IN MIST OR CLOUD. In clear weather the compass can be of use in checking your interpretation of the map but its greatest use is at night or when visibility is limited by mist. You will be so often caught by one or the other that a knowledge of its correct use is essential. The difference between magnetic north, that is the north to which the compass needle points, and true north, is shown on the margin of the map. Allow for this.

Remember never to have any iron or steel near the compass when taking a bearing.

In featureless country, darkness or mist a party of three can keep direction by walking in line at intervals of ten paces. The direction of the line should be set by compass bearing. The last man carries the compass and directs the party. He should always keep the leader in line with the middle man. Any deviations from this by the leader are corrected by orders from the last man, e.g., "One pace to the left" or "Two paces to the right." Periodically a fresh compass check should be made.

Such a technique is rarely necessary in Britain in daylight. Most hill districts are provided with recognisable natural features and practice will make their identification by the map possible, especially if the route has been well studied before setting out.

If mist or cloud threaten make a quick restudy of the ground and map as far ahead as you can see. It will be a very thick fog that does not then allow you to see and identify prominent features as you approach them on your compass bearing.

AT NIGHT. In a clear night the most convenient check on general direction is given by the Pole Star.

If the darkness is dense a compass should be used in the same way as in mist; and here again pre-knowledge gained by study of the route on the map and on the ground before dusk closes in is the best guide.

GENERAL. When route finding for any reason begins to grow difficult the leader should consider any suggestions put forward by other members of the party and explain to them why he chooses the line he adopts. After that the party must obey orders, and the leader must not allow any talkative or opinionated member of the party afterwards to unsettle his decision.

CHANGE THE ROUTE TO SUIT THE GROUND. As soon as the first clear view over the ground ahead is obtained and later whenever a wide viewpoint is reached check again the routes you chose overnight from the map against the actual country. Modify your line accordingly. It may be that there is a stretch of boggy ground or of rough going which was unmarked on the map and which can better be avoided by an easy deviation.

In climbing a mountain the ridges offer usually the best way, the sides of the mountain will give more difficult and rougher going, and the gullies and little valleys will be boggy, hummocky, abrupt and rough.

Something about various types of hill country is given below. In general avoid scree, rocks, gullies and swampy places. Keep to the bare turf and the high ridges where you can see your line clear ahead.

Use paths and tracks wherever you can—they take the quickest line and generally the most sensible line, but make sure they are not sheep tracks—sheep seldom go the way that a man wants to go.

In precipitous mountains never attempt to follow a stream down unless you can see the whole of its course to easier ground, or unless you have previously been up the same way. In British mountains it is usually easier and safer to follow the ridges. For much the same reason never start running down a steep hillside unless you can see all your way down. It is often difficult to stop quickly, and the slope in the section you cannot see may run out over a crag invisible above.

G R A S S. Short grass gives the most pleasant and easiest walking. Grass slopes are usually the easiest way up a hill, and may be descended rapidly with safety—providing you can see all the way down, and have strong ankles and nailed boots.

Steep grass may get coated with ice or thin snow in winter and should then be avoided both in ascent and descent; it can give a nasty and long fall.

B R A C K E N. Bracken should be avoided in summer as it makes walking very laborious and is full of heat, damp and insects. On rocks and steep hillsides it is treacherous to use as a handhold, as it is very brittle and the roots come out easily.

H E A T H E R is much better for climbing as the plant is tough and not easily uprooted. But heather-covered slopes of boulders are a nightmare.

S C R E E. Scree is the name given to steep slopes of loose stones or rocks. In general in this country scree provides a safe if rather tiresome way up a mountain-side when it is large and a rapid way down if it is small.

In ascent it is preferable to avoid scree and to climb grass slopes. If you want to run down scree without a cut or twisted ankle, you must wear boots, hold your legs stiff and drive the heels well in. Large scree should be avoided in a descent.

The following are the safety rules:—

(*a*) Climb or descend as near as you can in line abreast.

(*b*) If your scree slope is shut in by steep rocks, as in a gully, and you have to follow in line, keep close together so that stones dislodged have no time to get up speed and become dangerous to the members of the party following.

R O C K S. The most difficult ways up British hills are up the rocks. Rocks are best avoided by the walker and left to the rock climber. Sometimes human nature cannot resist scrambling up a crag, as the shorter route. If so, remember that your safety lies in good foothold, not in hanging on by your hands. Choose each foothold and test it before standing on it.

To avoid slipping, or dislodging stones, place each foot as neatly as if you were dancing, and don't shift about on it when your weight comes on it. Think ahead exactly how you will make each lift or movement; and never let yourself get hurried, or try to rush it because you begin to think it is unsafe.

There are few places in British hills where you cannot avoid descending rocks—there is usually an easy way round. Never start down a crag where the whole way down cannot be seen or where you find it necessary to drop more than once from the hands.

STONES. Do not knock stones down steep hillsides on to the rest of the party, or over a cliff, the bottom of which is invisible. Never throw stones over a cliff or a steep slope. On rocks be extra careful if the footholds have loose stones on them. Do not assume because you can hear or see no one else that there is no one else on the mountain or even near you. Other parties are probably quieter than your own.

BOG. Upon all hills there are large stretches of boggy ground. These are rarely dangerous but they should always be avoided as they are heavy going and will tire the party needlessly.

RIVERS, STREAMS AND LAKES. Most hillside streams are easy to cross; but always cross carefully and choose the easiest place. In attempting to cross dry shod you may be tempted to make too long a jump and slip. The rivers in the main valleys should be crossed by bridges—especially after heavy rain when they are in spate. In a strongly flowing river it is extremely difficult to wade safely in water above hip level as the bottom is usually rocky and uneven. A detour is more pleasant than a ducking on a cold day.

Quite a number of the mountain lakes have steep hillsides rising straight out of them. It is easier to fall in than to climb out. Always walk carefully when traversing the hillside above a lake especially in mist or at dusk.

FENCES AND FARMERS. Do not break down fences, loosen walls or climb over gates.

Always close gates after use.

Do not walk over growing crops or sown land.

If by accident a fence or a wall is damaged see that the damage is repaired before you go on. Farmers are busy men who need our help more than our hindrance.

RESTS AND HALTING PLACES. The leader should decide when the time has come for a halt and how long it should last. Choose a place sheltered from the wind. Put on spare clothing. Try and rest completely: relax. Ease the feet by removing boots and pulling up socks and stockings. Any blisters or hint of soreness should be dealt with immediately. A piece of Elastoplast put over the rubbed skin in time will prevent blister developing or getting worse.

Eat slowly: drink sparingly and in sips. Do not start off again until all the party have finished eating and re-packing.

It is generally safe to drink from mountain streams in Britain provided the water is clear and running and does not smell or taste. Always taste water before drinking any. However thirsty drink only in moderation or better still merely wash the mouth out.

Do not drink from valley streams and rivers, or from any that are below human dwellings, farm buildings or cattle shelters.

Make certain also that there is not a dead sheep in the water higher up.

During rests the opportunity can be taken to change the rucksacks round so that all do their fair share of carrying. It is up to the leader to arrange this. Of course everyone need not carry the rucksack for the same time—the stronger may be handicapped by a longer carry, particularly anyone who makes a nuisance of himself by always sprinting.

WEATHER. Rain is uncomfortable; but so long as you keep going and don't halt the drenching can do no harm. There is even a moist-warm pleasure in feeling you can't get wetter!

Mist complicates route finding. All the distances you think you have fixed look different through it, and all nearer features, rocks, and so on, are magnified confusingly and look like mountains. In thick mist we soon lose our sense of direction and start wandering. You will have to slow up and allow far more time to finding the right route; and you will probably have to shorten the whole expedition to suit.

Wind is another factor you cannot neglect. A head wind will take off the pace and add hours to your estimate for the day. A cold wind especially with sleet in it will drive you off your line and can reduce the stamina and endurance of your party more than any other cause. Look out for this before you start and see that spare clothing is taken by everyone.

Wind, if you have noted its constant direction, can help to guide you in thick mist if you keep it on the same cheek. But you must not assume that it is blowing from a constant quarter except on open moorland. In valleys and hollows and along the edges of cliffs gusts may come from very different quarters. And a point to remember is, not to skirt the top of a cliff too closely in a wind however good your balance: mountain eddies swirl up fiercely enough to blow the heaviest of us off our footing.

Snow in hills must be treated with great caution. If it is under foot and soft under sunshine, it will make very heavy going and will add many hours to a hill walk: under foot and hard, it makes good going until the slope gets steep, when it can be very treacherous. Unless you are experienced a slide on hard snow is often impossible to stop and may shoot you over broken rocks or even a cliff. Falling snow in hills is likely to turn to a blizzard; and there is no worse enemy to fight through. If you are caught stick close together and make for the nearest valley with a road or path down it.

PACE. It is a common mistake to go too fast at the beginning of the day. See to it that the start is slow, working comfortably up to an almost mechanical swing-out. In this way the party will have plenty of energy left for any special efforts needed during the day, and for the long final trudge. If the rest of the party complains that the pace is too slow you are probably setting it about right.

Keep the pace steady throughout the day and keep going. Make good restful halts when you stop; but don't stop often; thirty unnoticed minutes lost in dawdling mean a priceless half hour cut off your daylight at the end. Don't encourage casual dropping out except at the arranged halts, it breaks the rhythm unconsciously for all the rest and slackens the effort all round.

Uphill, aim at an easy swing-up of the leg, but set the foot down precisely. Do not spring off the toes alone. Wherever possible set the whole sole of the foot on the ground, and horizontally; you can often manage this even on very steep slopes by ascending in zig-zags or by placing the heel on a stone or a tuft.

When you wish to increase the speed do so by lengthening the stride, not by hurrying it. Breathe rhythmically as best suits your stride and the angle you are ascending. On steep angles ease the effort for lungs and legs by balancing a little forward. If a walker can still whistle or sing to himself while he is going steadily uphill he is going within his pace. Do not race up the last slopes when the summit is in sight.

In descending flex the knees, and keep the weight well forward. Do not go so fast that you begin to feel the jar, nor fast at all unless your boots fit so well that they don't bruise your toes.

It is for the leader to see that his party keeps together and that there are no stragglers. He must moderate the over-keen so that the weaker members are not left perpetually tailing behind. There is nothing makes a tired man feel his tiredness more than being left to chase along behind alone on a long return. If tempers get worn as they may on a wet and windy trudge do not allow splitting up, and as soon as you get on to track or road, see that slow and fast swing into stride together: song can help immensely at these times.

Observation

The pleasure of hill walking is not limited, as a minority of walkers would seem to think, to the enjoyment we derive from feeling physically fit, from our own trained and rhythmical movements, and from noting how many miles and feet we can traverse in a day. It depends far more upon what we learn to see and understand with our senses of the tremendous scenery through which we pass, of the great valleys and the cliffs, the clouds and shadows on the hillside, the flowers and the birds, and the sounds of wind and falling water. My purpose in this chapter is to give just the minimum of practical knowledge needed for a safe start: so that you can extend your walking confidently into rough hill country, and after very little practice feel free there to observe and to enjoy without having to go on paying too much attention to your next step or the line ahead. Because once you have learned to observe closely you will find that you choose your line and your next step rightly and without knowing it, while you can give your whole conscious attention to all the new wonders of mountains you are discovering round you. You will find then that our hills hold a new world of pleasure kept particularly till you came.

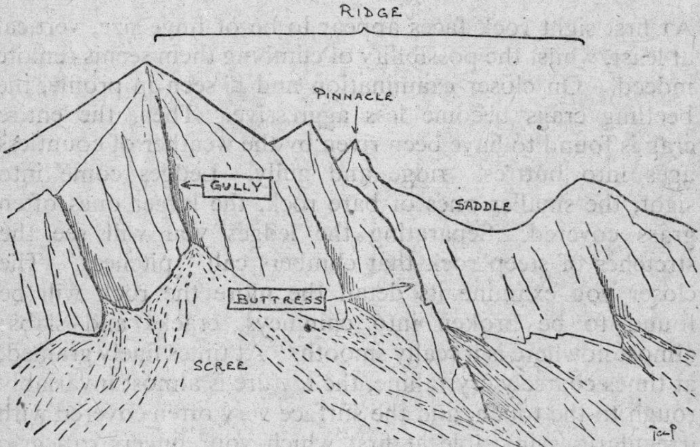

FIG. 12—THE MAIN FEATURES OF MOUNTAINS

Chapter 4

ROCK CLIMBING

At first sight rock faces appear to be of huge size, vertical at least, whilst the possibility of climbing them seems remote indeed. On closer examination and if seen in profile, the beetling crags become less aggressive. Then, the entire crag is found to have been riven by the weather of countless ages into buttress, ridge and gully. Ledges come into sight, the smaller ones of bare rock, the larger ones often grass covered. Separating the ledges you will see the stretches of steep rock that climbers call "pitches." The closer you examine its detail the more the rock will be found to be broken into chimneys, cracks and slabs: almost nowhere is it really smooth. At times finely grained, at times coarsely crystalline, the texture is almost invariably rough to the touch, and the surface very often covered with irregularities invisible at first which your fingers can grip and your feet can use as holds. By the number and size of the ledges, the steepness of the connecting pitches, the frequency and size of holds you can, generally speaking, decide as to the difficulty of a cliff. The fewer the ledges and the steeper the rock the harder will be the climb.

In its development the sport of climbing followed certain stages and it is suggested here that you can build up a sound technique by pursuing a course which will take you through the same stages. After the early days of climbing along the obvious ridges, steeper ribs and buttresses were attempted by adapting alpine technique. After this for a time the exploration turned into the great rifts and gullies. In gullies you find steep breaks or pitches, but often with comfortable ledges between them. The pitches may be caves, formed by huge jammed blocks, or they may be chimneys and cracks, and occasionally even smooth slabs.

The comparative shelter of the walled gullies gave confidence and enabled the technique to develop until a very high standard indeed was reached in this type of climbing.

As men gained confidence, and found it easier and safer to

FIG. 13—IN BALANCE ON THE FEET

stand in balance on their feet upon small holds, rather than to cling on to them by their hands, the best men of each decade ventured round more corners and climbed steeper slabs; until even sheer walls were found to be possible. With growing confidence, and the improving technique that came from it, climbers learned not to be afraid of "exposure": by this is meant the exposure of the climber over some considerable drop, the realisation of which will try his nerves, in his early stages at least, and so hamper his standard of performance. We now know that we can get accustomed to any exposure at any height;

that practice begets confidence, and that confidence produces easy and bold movement. So that a climber now expects to climb to the limit of his ability, however exposed the pitch may be.

These were the stages of climbing history. And a beginner cannot do better than take them in the same order: from easy ridges (for balance, neat footwork and rope technique) to gullies; so to slabs and cracks, and finally to sheer walls.

Climbing Company

I repeat, because it is important, that, for your first climbing expeditions, it is far better to arrange to go with someone who has climbed before and can show you how to. More is learned in one hour from a climber than in days from reading books.

If however you have to start with someone who knows as little as yourself, you must take very great care indeed. Climbing is not difficult to do; but, unlike other sports, it is very dangerous if done badly, and you may have to pay for ignorance or for a commonplace mistake as a beginner by a serious injury.

Remember next, that the rope is not used to help you up a climb; and that it cannot prevent the leader on a climb falling. Its only use is to reduce the serious or fatal results of a slip or fall, once it has taken place.

Again, from the moment you start up a climb, you have two immediate responsibilities. One is never to slip yourself; and, two, is to be ready at every instant to check with the rope a slip by your companion, no matter how good you may think him.

Balance

The whole art of climbing is built upon balance, balance of the body above the feet, in an erect position. Legs and feet must learn to do most of the work: hands and arms serve mainly to assist balance and assure stability. This rule has exceptions, as when you need a special effort of arm strength to overcome a particular problem. By standing comfortably on the feet, or a single toe, and using the hands, or a finger, as retaining grips, you can keep your body balancing well clear of the rock; and so make sure of noticing all available holds and the best method and order of using them. It is far easier to see ledges and stances, ahead or to

FIG. 14—LEGS AND FEET DO THE WORK

left and right, from a free erect position, and your upward progress will not then be checked by friction of your clothes on the rock. This controlled and balanced progress from foothold to foothold is very economical of muscular energy, and it enables you to keep a reserve of strength in hand for the wrestles with awkward passages where your whole body may have to come into play.

Strength is not important in climbing. Rushing,

scrabbling or muscling up are merely dangerous. Neatness, coolness, the settling beforehand just what holds you will use, and how, and then making the movement deliberately and smoothly, are what make the great climber.

Weather

Weather has a great effect on a climber and on how he climbs on a particular day. In bright sunshine with dry rocks you can give of your best, and enjoy your climbing up to the limit of your powers. On a wet day with damp mist around everything, the rock soon grows greasy, friction is reduced and your fingers are quickly chilled, so that if the rock is at all steep and exposed your standard may be reduced to half or less of your performance in good weather. A strong cold or wet wind upon your cliff will have much the same effect.

Choice of Climb

In choosing your region or your cliff to begin upon, better choose one where you have some knowledge of the locality and have previously walked. This will increase your confidence. A crag with a sunny side and out of the wind will be found more comfortable on which to begin operations.

It is the custom for beginners to start on well-known climbs on popular cliffs. This helps because the routes will be found well marked with nail scratches and the passage of many climbers will have removed loose holds. On these climbs too, belays have been cleaned out and will be obvious on every ledge. All this allows you to concentrate entirely on the actual climbing and rope management and will save you false starts or getting off the sound route.

Guide books

The rock climbing guides issued by the various climbing clubs will be found valuable;* firstly in the choice of your

*See Chapter 11.

crag, secondly of your climb. Climbs will be found grouped under several headings, usually somewhat as follows:—

1. Moderate.
2. Difficult.
3. Very difficult.
4. Severe.
5. Very severe.

The grading assumes dry rocks and reasonably good conditions. You may trust to the information given, particularly in the grading of the easier climbs.

You will see that first is given the total length of the climb together with its grading. This last is nearly always the standard of the hardest pitch on the climb and is not an estimated average. The descriptive detail of the climb is given in pitches, that is the stretches of climbing between belays and stances. So far as easier climbs are concerned it may be assumed that belays and sound ledges appear together.

Having chosen a climb and identified the start you can prepare to ascend it.

Rope and Knots

Put on the rope and remember that rope (as distinct from alpine line) is alone recommended for beginners. Sixty feet is about the right length for two climbers, while often a hundred foot length will suffice for three. A bowline (Fig. 15) is always used for the end knot, preferably secured by one or two half-hitches of the free end tied round the waist loop. The middle man may choose either a bowline on a bight (Fig. 17) or an ordinary overhand knot (Fig. 16), the latter being the simpler to remember and tie.

Definitions

Before we go any further we must define some of the terms we use.

ANCHOR. This is a projection or other feature of the cliff to which the rope can be firmly tied. An inserted peg is an artificial anchor.

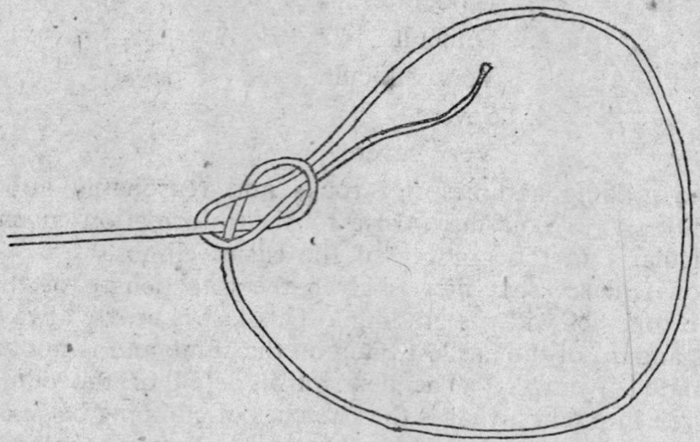

FIG. 15—THE BOWLINE KNOT

THE ACTIVE ROPE. This is the rope tied to the waist of the climber who is moving.

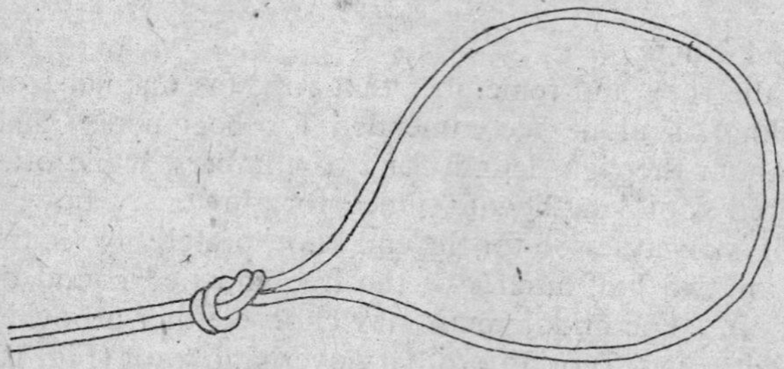

FIG. 16—THE ORDINARY OVERHAND KNOT

THE INACTIVE ROPE. This is the rope between climbers who are not moving—for instance between the second and third of the party while the leader is leading, or between the first and second while the last man is moving.

STANCE. A stance is any place on a cliff where you can stand comfortably in balance on your feet without using your hands.

BELAY. In the simple case, this is the action of fastening the rope round an anchor to safeguard a stance, or the moving climber. This subject is dealt with in detail later.

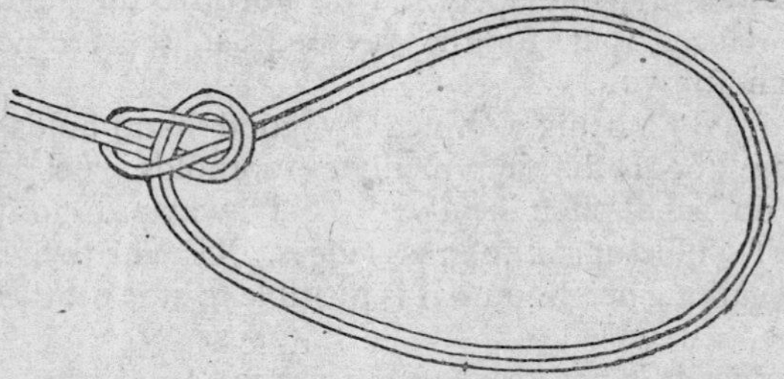

FIG. 17—THE BOWLINE ON THE BIGHT

INDIRECT BELAY. This is a belay made by using the inactive rope or an unused part of the active rope in such way that the spring of a human body may be interposed to supplement the strength of the active rope in the case of the moving climber falling.

DIRECT BELAY. This is a belay made with the active rope. With the cordage at present generally used, direct belays are unsound because the rope will break in the event of the leader falling.

The Start of the Climb

Now prepare for your work. Weigh up the climb as far as you can see, noting the likely stances and the general trend of the route, together with any obvious landmarks.

Having decided where the route must go, the next problem is to follow it. Before starting up each separate pitch of the climb you should examine the rock ahead in detail, and note the ledges likely to serve as resting places. Then, following the line of the best holds, make a careful and deliberate course up the pitch. Keep cool. If in real doubt do not hesitate to descend and have a rest before making another try. If you have moved in a calculated way descent will almost always turn out to be less strenuous than ascent. Do not be discouraged if the solution is not found at the first attempt: and do not give up the climb until convinced that, for the day at least, the problem is too much for you.

Try to avoid being tempted by good hand-holds into forgetting about the intermediate footholds you noted. Try to do each pitch neatly; avoid awkward positions and don't scuffle up on to grass ledges. Use the rock holds to go on gaining height until it is possible to step neatly on to the ledge.

Sometimes it is necessary to use a knee on a ledge or on other intermediate hold; but these places become rarer with practice. Often such knee use interferes with the next sequence of movements, in any case it probably prevents continuous clear view of all holds.

On the leader reaching a stance with a convenient anchor, he should tell you as second man of this by calling down "Right," "I'm there" or "I'm through." This is not to relieve your feelings of anxiety, but to warn you so that by the time he has belayed himself and starts to take in the slack of the rope you are ready to start at once.

Belaying

On his arrival at a stance the leader should at once look around for an anchor with which to secure the party. Anything may be used which gives a secure anchor for the rope, from a sound knob of rock to the threading of the rope behind a stone jammed in a crack or chimney. Occasionally an anchor is obtained by tying oneself to a detached block on a ledge: naturally it must be large enough to have sufficient inertia or wedged well enough to resist any shock likely to be laid on it.

The suggested way of belaying is, first to choose a spike (the anchor) as high as is reasonably accessible preferably above shoulder height. Then taking the rope running from your waist knot, lay it just taut over the notch behind

FIG. 18—THE PROPER BELAY FOR THE LEADER

the knob of rock. Bring the rope back and tuck a bight of it through your waist rope. With the bight make an overhand knot over the two parts of the rope, that is the one running from your waist knot to the anchor and the other which comes from the anchor and is used to make the bight on your waist rope. This belay is called the proper belay and is a fixed belay always associated with a stance.

It is probably unnecessary to say that the test of any belay is that it will do its job, i.e., in the event of a fall that it will remain a secure anchor for those members of the party who are tied to it. Therefore every belay used should be considered from this point of view. The man putting the

FIG. 19—THE PROPER BELAY AS USED BY THE SECOND

belay on should consider what will happen to it and to him if the leader or the man who is actually moving falls off. It is very easy to put on a belay which superficially appears a very good one and to find when it comes to a real test that it is quite useless and in the wrong position to ensure the safety of the party. This lesson can unfortunately only be proved in the event. Very few people can imagine the nature of the jerk on the belayed man when a climber falls off until they have actually experienced it. It is very noticeable too that once this has happened to a man, he is very much more careful about his belays afterwards.

When the leader is anchored, he should at once take in the slack of the rope, coiling it neatly until all the free rope has been absorbed. Then he should call to you to "come on," placing the coil of rope where it will not be in the way of future movements. The rope to you he runs under his outside arm, round his back and in over the inside shoulder. He grips it with both hands one on each side of his body. As you advance he hauls in the slack and keeps the rope taut, but not tight. On your joining your leader at his stance, you change places. You anchor yourself securely to the rock and pay out the rope over one shoulder, down the back and under the other arm to your leader as he goes ahead up the next pitch. You should always keep a few feet of slack in the rope so that if the leader takes one or two quick steps together, he is not jerked.

You should make a firm habit of belaying securely on every stance; never trust to luck because it looks easy.

Holds

The main types of holds are as follows:—

A STRAIGHT PULL UP. This is a hold over which the fingers can curl as over the rung of a ladder in a comforting manner and on which the whole weight can be put for a straight hoist.

MANTELSHELF. This too is a horizontal hold, but not incut; so that the fingers cannot curl over it but only lie flat upon the top. It is consequently more difficult to pull up on and there may be some tricky balancing in the final stages of the movement especially if the cliff behind the hold rises steeply.

UNDERCUT. Occasionally one finds a hold like the pull up first described but with the incut on the underside instead of on top. This kind of hold is very useful for maintaining balance on a steep cliff as one can pull the weight of the body in towards the cliff; but naturally, no direct upward lift can be obtained from it.

PRESSURE. Many holds which are unsuitable for direct pulls are extremely satisfactory to press up on. One type of such hold is illustrated (Fig. 20).

SIDE PRESSURE. It is often possible to correct and ensure balance by side pressure against vertical ribs or corners of rock. Some cliffs present holds of this type almost to the exclusion of holds of normal character. A case of such a cliff is Lliwedd in North Wales (Fig. 21).

INCUTS FOR FEET. An incut hold can be much more useful for the feet than for the hands since a nail gets an adequate grip on a hold which is too small for even the strongest fingers. In using such small incuts boots often have an advantage over rubbers. This is particularly true of the East Wall of Idwal Slabs in North Wales and on similar rock in other districts.

LARGE HOLDS. Large holds in general lead to bad technique and it is not a good notion to take beginners on cliffs covered with large holds. It is better to teach them balance climbing on less steep cliffs with smaller holds.

LOOSE ROCK. In an ideal world no holds on loose rock would be used at all; in other words the place would be shunned and climbers would not go there. However, very good climbing cliffs have their patches of loose rock, and it is therefore necessary for climbers to know how to deal with them. Most loose rock holds can be used securely if used in one particular direction. They should be carefully inspected before use to decide upon the best

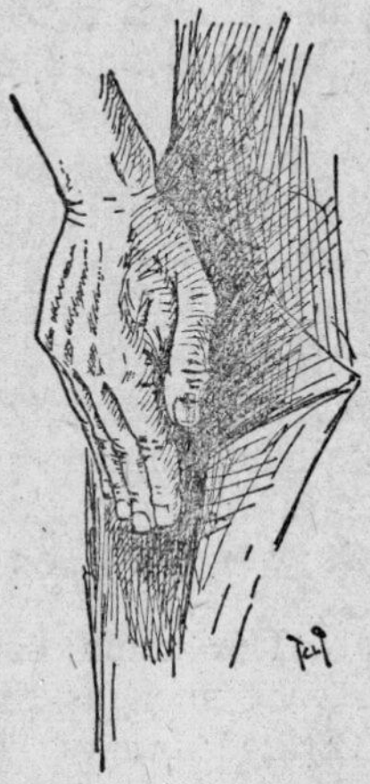

FIG. 20—A PRESSURE HOLD

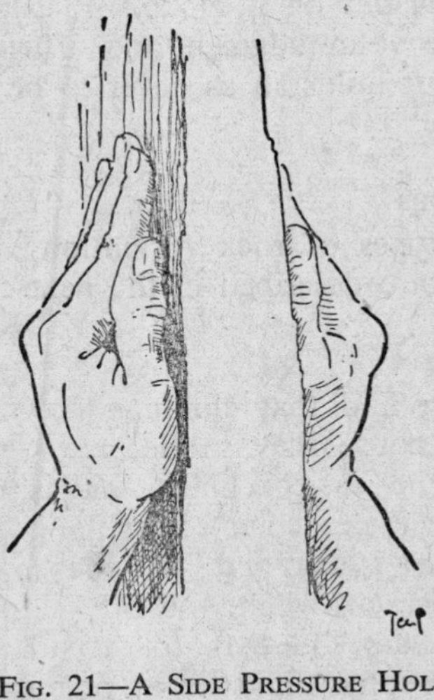

FIG. 21—A SIDE PRESSURE HOLD

way of holding them. On no account should you ever make a straight pull outward on a loose hold.

Even on popular climbs loose stones are met with. In gullies the top of each pitch often consists of a slope of debris. Great care should be taken to avoid sending down even a single stone. Once more, you will find neat balance on the feet an asset, for an upright position is less likely to cause stonefalls than an all-fours attitude. In addition, you must be careful in handling the rope, so that it does not catch under and send down any stones. If, in spite of every care, stone is dislodged, give warning at once to whoever is, or may be, down below.

BRITTLE ROCK. The same consideration applies to brittle rock. On rock such as the soft sandstone of Harrison's rocks at Eridge and of Helsby, the dolomite of Brassington and Harboro' and some of the Scottish sandstone of the Torridon and Dundonnell hills, a small hold although part of the mountain will break off if the whole weight is put on it alone. In such circumstances you should use your judgment and distribute your weight between all your holds so as never to be depending on a single frail one.

Rock Formations

The different types of rock formation and the ways of climbing them are described in the next chapter.

Climbing Down

Beginners often find that climbing down is harder than climbing up because they cannot see with their toes or heels. Upon the easier climbs this is not so, because much less effort is needed to lower the body from hold to hold than to raise it over the same rocks. Most chimneys also and many cracks where you can see the side walls are much easier to descend than to ascend. Of course you may experience some difficulty at first in correctly interpreting the oblique view of the holds for your feet with which you have to be satisfied. But practice overcomes this, and once mastered, the effortless descent of easy rocks has its own special pleasure.

With experience, it will be found easier to descend difficult rocks if you turn sideways or even face outwards rather than turn in towards the rock, and if you only turn into a face inwards position when the rock becomes really steep. So long as you face outwards or sideways you can see the holds ahead and adjust yourself easily to them. But when you face in to the rock you can no longer see the holds below you; and descent becomes tentative and slow.

Joining the Rope

If the party consists of more than two, and the single rope is not long enough, two ropes will have to be used. In this case always tie one rope only round the waist and knot the other to the waist loop so formed. On no account should a man tie the two ropes round his waist independently. The fisherman's bend (Fig. 22) is a good knot to use for the purpose.

Loose Coils

If for convenience one member of the party has to carry some coils of the climbing rope the coils should be knotted at both ends to his waist loop so that if he slips the coils do not tighten and strangle him.

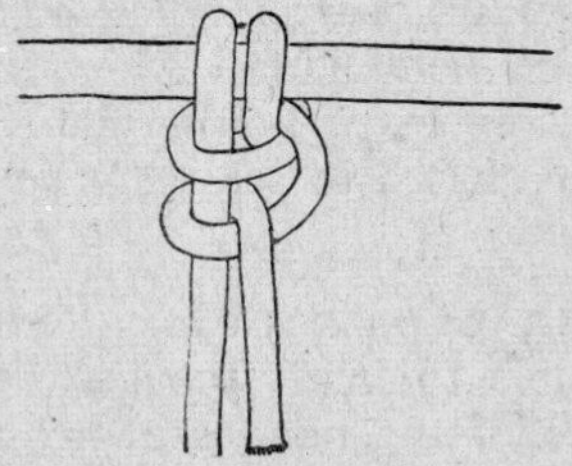

FIG. 22—THE FISHERMAN'S BEND

Chapter 5

MORE ADVANCED ROCK CLIMBING

Here we need some additional definitions:—

ABSEIL — RAPPEL — ROPE DOWN. These are the German, French and English terms for the same operation—letting oneself down a cliff using a doubled rope. The method is described in detail later (see page 76).

THE PRUSIK KNOT OR FRICTION HITCH. This is a new and very useful hitch which is used for attaching a subsidiary rope or sling to the main rope. It has the property of not slipping along the main rope when weight is put on the sling; while it is possible to push it along the main rope.

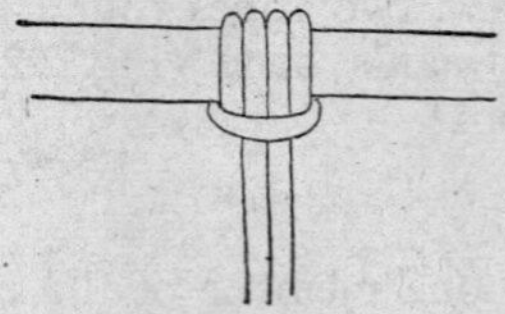

FIG. 23—THE FRICTION HITCH

Advanced Rock Climbing

There are some additional climbing techniques of which knowledge can be helpful and which I describe below; also some special types of holds. Before first using any of them you are advised to see them demonstrated by an experienced climber.

JAMMED FIST HOLDS. In a crack of the right width it is possible to insert the fist and then clench it, so that the sides of the hand are pressed firmly against the sides of the crack. This is a most satisfactory hold and the whole weight can quite confidently be put on it, providing the crack is a suitable one.

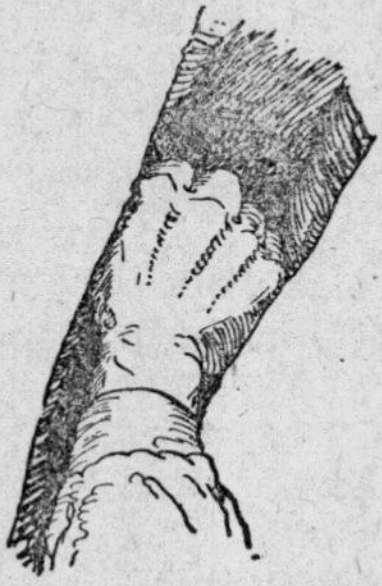

FIG. 24—THE JAMMED FIST HOLD

JAMMED HAND HOLDS. This can be used in narrower cracks where the fist as a hold cannot find room. The fingers of the hand are pressed against one side of the crack and the back of the hand against the other side. This is a very useful hold in rough-sided cracks but it entails a much greater strain on the fingers than the fist hold.

FIG. 25—THE JAMMED HAND HOLD

JAMMED FOOT HOLDS. In cracks of the right width the feet can be jammed by inserting them and twisting them. This is a like technique to the jammed hand but it is less precise.

PURE FRICTION. These are the holds found upon gritstone and Torridonian sandstone and sometimes on rhyolite and granite where propulsion can only be obtained by laying the hand or foot flat against the rock and pressing on it.

Methods of Climbing

In climbing steep slabs and walls, on small holds, balanced movement is vital. You cannot stop for long on such

FIG. 26—BACKING UP

holds without great strain; and you must plot your moves ahead—if possible, two moves ahead—up any severe section, so that you can maintain rhythm and balance while moving. On an overhang in particular, it pays to work out every movement and hold up the whole section beforehand, since you must not check once you have started such a severe passage.

Chimneys

A chimney is a crack wide enough to get into, and it can be climbed by a number of different methods.

BY BACKING UP. According to the width of the chimney set your feet or knees against one wall and your back against the other. You are then jammed. To move up press downward with one foot against the back wall

FIG. 27—BACKING UP—THE RESTING POSITION

under you, or with the hands against the same wall at hip level keeping one foot pressed against the opposite wall, your shoulders then come clear of the rock for an upward movement. The farther you are inside the chimney the greater the friction and the greater therefore your security ;

but since movement is your object as much as safety, it is usually better to compromise and come partly out of the chimney into freer climbing.

STRADDLING. Face into the chimney and set one foot and one hand on either wall, or possibly take hand-

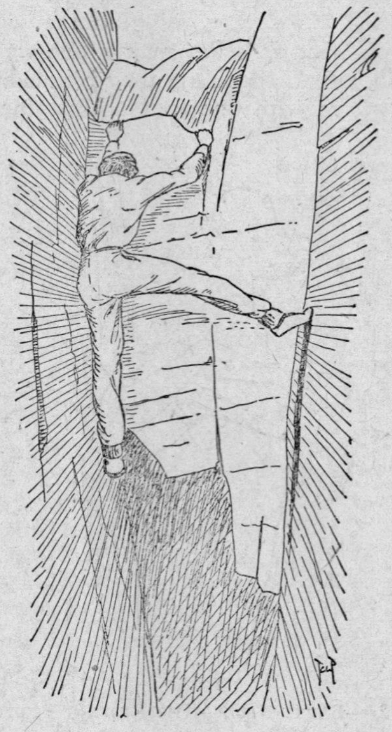

FIG. 28--STRADDLING

holds in the back of the chimney as in the illustration. The feet move up on incut or pressure holds alternately. This is less strenuous than backing up as it uses any holds there may be, and is the expert's preferred way.

WRIGGLING. In very narrow chimneys or chimney-cracks straddling and backing up are both impossible, and the only thing to do is to get the body into the chimney and climb it by wriggling and hand pressures on the walls. An example is the Monolith Crack on the Gribin of Cwm Idwal.

FIG. 29—THE LAYBACK

Cracks

These are fissures in the rocks too narrow to jam into. They are climbed:

(i) BY HOLDS on the edges if these are adequate.

(ii) BY A LAYBACK. Where the crack is in a corner, and with a sharp edge, you grip the edge, set your feet against the rock, and lift against your foot pressure. This is strenuous, and calls for power because your arms are carrying more than your dead weight.

(iii) BY JAMMING HANDS AND FEET. For a crack of say 3″-5″ width where there are no ordinary pull

FIG. 30—JAMMING HANDS AND FEET

holds. The jammed fist gives a most satisfactory hold and the whole weight can easily be supported from it if the crack is of the right width and the rock of correct texture.

It is the discovery of the effectiveness of these special techniques which gives one of the distinctive pleasures to rock climbing.

Climbing in Bad Weather

Bad or cold weather increases the difficulty considerably in the case of any climb with many small or friction holds. The dangers of numb hands and fingers are considerable in frosty or wet weather and mitts or cotton gloves should be worn so long as the climb permits. These are of little use, however, if the rocks are wet, and mechanical methods of warming the hands may have to be used. In any case before any move, doubtful because of its difficulty, is attempted you should make sure that the fingers are warm and have feeling in them, even if the process slows down the climb. Cases have occurred where the leader has lost all feeling in his fingers without appreciating it and fallen off in consequence.

Leading Through

A pleasant way for two expert climbers of approximately equal ability is to " lead through." In this method each man leads alternate pitches. One man having led the first pitch belays himself and brings up his second. The second man then carries straight on and up the next pitch. On reaching a stance he belays and brings up his second, who in turn, becomes the leader and carries straight on again.

An Alternative Method of Roping

A method of roping that may become popular is the following:—The main climbing rope has an eye, with a metal insert spliced in it at either end. Each climber has a separate rope sling round his waist, and attaches the main rope to this by a snaplink and one of the eyes. Any middleman there may be attaches his waist-loop by a snaplink to a prusik-sling affixed to the main rope. The advantages of this method are that it is always easy to unrope, or to clear a tangle; that the main rope slides on the snaplink round your waist into positions easy for your climbing, and that the middleman can easily change his position on the main rope relatively to the end men—often a desirable matter.

Roping Down

Roping down is not an essential technique in this country;

FIG. 31—ROPING DOWN

but a knowledge of it is useful especially if you have to descend a climb in a hurry.

There are two main methods in use, the "classic" method and the "snaplink" method. In both methods the rope (or preferably lighter line) is passed round an anchor so that the two equal lengths hang down the desired line of descent. If the belay has sharp corners it is best to protect the rope against fraying by wrapping a handkerchief or paper round it where it crosses the sharp edges. Since the rope will have to be pulled round or jerked off from below when the operation is complete, make sure that there is no tendency to jam—on the other hand make certain that it is secure and will not " roll up " on the anchor. The last man but one when he has got down should test the freedom of the rope before the last man descends.

If there is doubt about the possibility of flicking or pulling the rope off when the descent has been accomplished, and to avoid the necessity of having to climb up again to retrieve the rope, use a sling round the anchor and thread the rope.

Before using the rope check that the ends are together, that they reach the stance below and that they hang untwisted and parallel to one another.

Before starting the coat collar should be turned up to protect the neck from the rubbing of the rope.

THE CLASSIC METHOD. The doubled rope is taken in the left hand and the climber stands astride it facing the belay, so that it passes between his legs from front to back. The double rope is then taken behind the right thigh up across the front of the body and over the left shoulder—front to back. The hanging rope is held in the right hand and the climber walks back down the cliff, keeping the body and the legs fairly straight and the feet about a yard apart horizontally.

The speed of descent is controlled by the position of the ropes held in the right hand. If there is a long length of rope hanging below or if the rope is wet, it will not slide easily over the shoulder and round the thigh and it will be necessary to ease the rope round by lifting it with the right hand. If it is found that there is a contrary tendency to go too fast the hanging ropes can be brought round to the front of the body, still in the right hand and pressed against the ropes in the left hand. The increased friction caused by contact between the two ropes and the larger length of rope in contact with the body will provide more than enough braking capacity.

The chief trouble with this method of roping down is in starting; if the cliff below is steep and the point of anchorage at the level of the stance, the rope has to be put on,above the level of the point of anchorage. The difficulty is to get the body into the correct position below the anchor and with the rope untangled and in the right place.

THE SNAPLINK METHOD. The difficulty may be made much less by using the snaplink method. A second sling and a snaplink are required. The legs are placed through the sling which is pulled to a position midway up the thighs. The snaplink is then used to join together the back and front of the slings between the legs. The doubled abseil rope is fixed as described above, passed through the snaplink and over the left shoulder from front to back. The hanging ropes are held in the right hand as before, the ropes from the anchorage in the left. Special care is needed to ensure that the ropes through the snaplink do not interfere with one another or tend to open the clip. This method like the first one should be practised in a safe place before it is tried on a cliff.

More about Belays

In the chapters on rock climbing and on snow and ice work, a good deal has already been said about belays and the importance of good belaying.

Good belaying is such a great part of the art of climbing, and particularly of rock climbing as we know it in this country, that I now propose to deal with it in detail.

In the past twenty years, rock climbing has developed

enormously, not only in the hands of the very expert but also among many thousands of moderate parties. This development has been made comparatively safe by the care taken by most parties in belaying, and the high technical development of the great climbers has only been possible because they have always treated belaying as a very serious matter indeed and devoted considerable time and thought to the development of its technique.

This chapter then is an endeavour to record the stage which this technique has now reached.

It is a commonplace on British cliffs that the man or woman who belays best also climbs the best. They also most certainly enjoy their climbing more. A leader will climb very much better than he otherwise would if he knows that his second is well anchored. As confidence is the only thing that makes the really hard climbs possible, anything that increases the climber's confidence increases his ability to climb rocks. None of the great modern climbs would have been done except for the development of this technique.

Most belaying on normal rock climbs is done by using the climbing rope, that is the rope joining members of the climbing party. In addition, as stated earlier, it has become the practice for the leader to carry a number of rope or line slings of suitable length. They should be long enough to go round a man's waist and be tied there.

In addition to normal belays as already described, there are also running belays which have a considerable application in advanced climbing.

Fixed anchors are used to secure any member of the party who is not moving so that he can pay out or take in the rope to the moving member of the party.

There are many kinds of fixed belays of which only one, the proper belay, has so far been dealt with (on page 61).

To illustrate the application of these various forms of belay I assume that they are being used by the second to safeguard the leader.

THE CAMBRIDGE ANCHOR. This is the most primitive form of fixed anchor and should only be used in cases where speed is essential. The anchor must be a firm bollard or spike above the level of the second. The second takes the inactive rope leaving his waist loop and coils it round the bollard a number of times without knotting it or tying it at all. It is not suitable on any bollard which is rounded.

THE PROPER BELAY. This has been described in Chapter 4 (page 61). It has the advantage that the loop can be made of the right length to suit the physical configuration of the stance, and if the bollard is firm the second is then absolutely safe from the very serious consequences of a fall on the part of his leader.

The same principle can be used even if the spike or bollard is not satisfactory for rope but would be for line if a line sling is employed. In this case the line sling is passed over the spike and tied back in one of the ways shown in the illustration.

THE OVERHAND KNOT BELAY. This is sometimes more suitable for use where the anchor spike is not directly above the stance but is displaced to one side. In such positions the second must assume that he will in fact be pulled off his stance and swing below his anchor. The overhand knot belay will ensure that if he does so, the belay will stay on. It consists of a loop tied in the inactive rope or the unused part of the active rope with an overhand knot and placed over the spike (Fig. 32).

It is of course mechanically weaker than the proper belay, but in many cases, where the anchor spike is not in a good position, the loop will stay on where the proper belay would not.

CHOCKSTONES. Chockstones may vary considerably in size from pebbles in thin cracks behind which even line can hardly be threaded to great boulders jammed in gullies weighing several tons. The method of tying on to them thus varies very considerably. With the small variety and with some large ones where the aperture behind the chockstones is still very small a line sling must be used, as this, particularly if it is neatly served at the end, will pass through the "eye" behind the chockstone where rope possibly cannot go. A tapered serving on the end of the

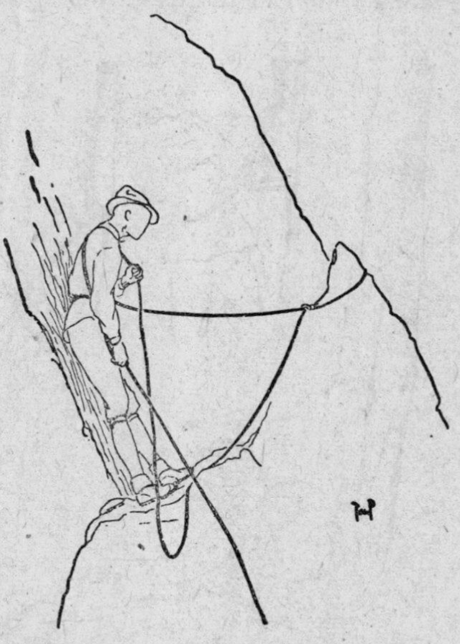

FIG. 32—THE OVERHAND KNOT BELAY

sling will further assist threading. The sling having been passed behind the chockstone should be knotted together and tied to the waist loop. Alternatively, you can tie on to the main rope leaving 7 or 8 ft. spare from your waist and this can be threaded and tied back to your waist loop. Alternatively, the main rope itself can be used, but to avoid untying it at the waist it is usually preferable for this to be threaded double. The whole belay is then an ugly and complicated one although undoubtedly very safe.

In a number of recent climbs the technique of the "inserted" chockstone belay has been employed. The climber carries or picks out by his stance loose pebbles or small stones and by trial and error finds one which will fit and jam securely in any available crack. The rope can then be threaded round in the usual way.

FIG. 33—THE USE OF CHOCKSTONES

This technique demands considerable skill and care because it is difficult always to test adequately that an inserted chockstone will stay in when the jerk of a falling body comes on it. As against this however one of the most famous and practically tested anchors in North Wales, that at the stance below the crux of Longland's climb on

Clogwyn du'r Arddu, was an inserted chockstone. If chosen and inserted with care they can be thoroughly safe and serve to guard a party where no natural anchor exists.

THE JAMMED KNOT. This is a further very specialized anchor of limited utility. Sometimes it definitely comes within the category of "psychological" belays, described below.

A simple overhand knot is tied in the inactive rope, either single or doubled according to circumstances and the knot jammed in a crack of suitable width and pulled down until it jams firmly. This belay would almost certainly come out nine times out of ten if used as a direct belay—if used as an indirect belay in the proper manner it will provide an adequate anchor for the second if he is on a good stance.

THE "PSYCHOLOGICAL" BELAY. This form of belay is mentioned for completeness and its use is not recommended. It uses an anchor which is fairly unlikely to be satisfactory, or no anchor at all. For example a number of spikes each of which are individually not sound may be used together as one anchor. This gives a "psychological" belay and an illusion of security which in turn may give sufficient confidence to enable the climb to be proceeded with, but will actually not be secure if a fall occurs. Such belays serve a useful function in climbs of a high standard, because they may be the means of giving the leader sufficient confidence to lead a difficult pitch safely, which he could not do if there was no belay at all. But there is never any need to use them on easier climbs and before using them the leader should think three times and ponder very seriously upon the ethical basis of his climbing and the safety of the party as a whole. The ordinary party would in such circumstances turn back and the editor of this book being less high principled might consider the use of a peg.

PEGS. Pegs are used as belays only where no other belays are available and there is a widespread feeling in this country that their use is unsporting and that a climb done with their use is not well done. In any case they are never left in the cliff, and must be removed by the second or last man as a point of honour. Luckily British rock, in general, does not encourage their use, and it is always necessary to check that they are driven in securely in a crack of the right width, and that a peg of the right type is used. This point is illustrated in Fig. 34. There are also illus-

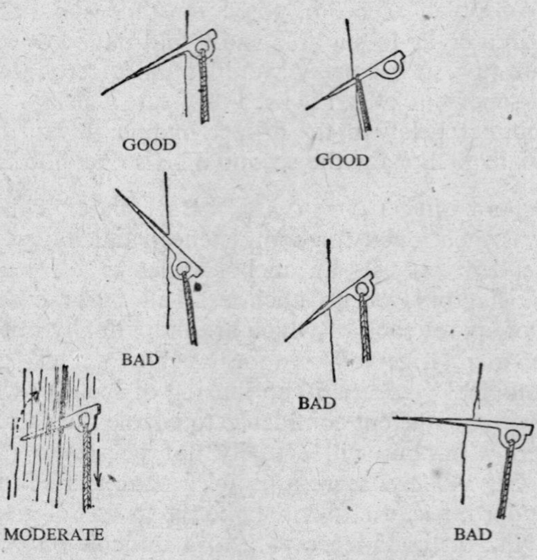

FIG. 34—THE USE OF PEGS

trated (Fig. 8) the whole range of pegs which could be bought in Great Britain before the war. It would be possible to carry one of each type to ensure that the most suitable kind was available if needed; actually most British climbers converted to their occasional use carried one only.

If the peg cannot be driven in right to the head, as it

should always be, it is better to tie the belaying rope direct to the peg close to the rock, rather than to use the peg ring which would unnecessarily increase the leverage.

It is usually not necessary to carry a hammer as small stones of the massive igneous rocks of this country make a good substitute and can be found near the scene of the crime.

RUNNING BELAYS. These are sliding belays on the active rope and are used to give a feeling of security to the leader before attempting a particularly difficult step, or on a long pitch where there are intermediate belays, but no intermediate stances to reduce the effective length of the lead. When the leader, who needs to carry a sling (or a peg) for the purpose, reaches such a belay, he puts a sling over it and threads the main rope through the sling, or through a snaplink attached to the sling, and then carries on with the pitch. The point to notice is that if he does fall off he will fall freely twice the distance between himself and the running belay, instead of twice the distance between himself and his second—a considerable increase in safety.

The second, however, in arranging his belay must recognize the fact that the first pull which may come on him will come in an upwards direction.

If snaplinks are not used, friction will be increased—and the active rope may partially jam—thus considerably increasing the leader's difficulty. More than one running belay can be used in a pitch if it is a very long one, or with more than one excessively difficult move, but each additional belay increases the likelihood of excessive friction and the desirability of using snaplinks.

The leader must also remember that the belays must be arranged so that they do not make the second's following him any more difficult: that is he should not expect the second to deviate from the easiest route to retrieve the slings or allow the rope whose direction is controlled by the position of the belays to come to the second in such a way that it gives him no support should it prove necessary, or protection if he should fall off.

Sometimes, however, the use of a running belay may substantially reinforce the confidence of the second without helping the leader much; in these cases the good leader would use them. Such a case is a pitch consisting of two

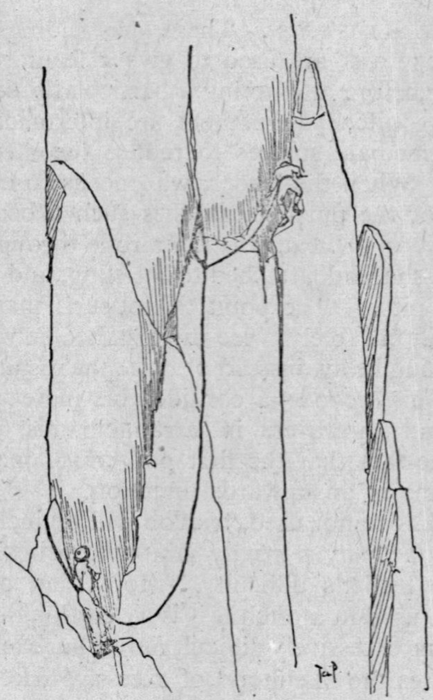

FIG. 35—A RUNNING BELAY TO SAFEGUARD THE LEADER

sections, a steep hard vertical section followed by an easier horizontal traverse. A running belay fixed at the top of the vertical section will safeguard the second against a bad swing. On another kind of pitch—a difficult traverse followed by a vertical section—a running belay at the end of the traverse may help the leader's confidence on the vertical section, but if the second gets into difficulties on the traverse he cannot be assisted or completely safeguarded by the leader.

A peg or any of the anchors used for securing stances

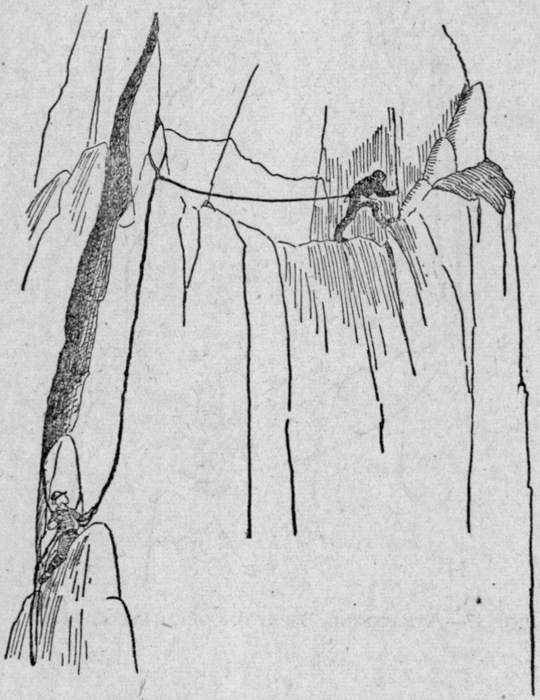

FIG. 36—A RUNNING BELAY TO HELP BOTH LEADER AND SECOND

can be used for anchoring the running belay. It is important that the second should recover the slings or pegs and bring them up to the leader, as he may wish to use them again. In any case it is bad form and bad climbing to leave such litter on a mountainside, as well as extravagant. In the Alps the position is rather different, and anyone who removes an essential peg may meet with local disfavour.

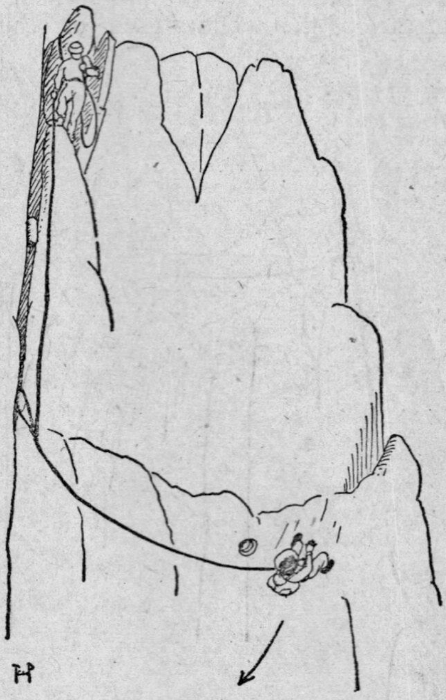

FIG. 37—A RUNNING BELAY INCORRECTLY APPLIED

Chapter 6

SNOW AND ICE

THIS chapter is mainly founded on Scottish experience, but it will apply to Cumberland, North Wales or elsewhere in England whenever conditions are favourable. These mountains can provide an adequate training ground for elementary snow and ice technique, but you must remember that, in the north, the harder the mountains become with snow and ice and storm conditions, the shorter also grow the daylight hours allowed for us to climb them, and the more bitter and threatening become the longer hours of darkness supposing we are benighted. So that, while the difficulties of snow and ice work may be less than those found in the Alps, the conditions under which we tackle them are much more risky.

In view of this, and the chances of a dull day turning to blizzard, a party starting on a big northern precipice should take plenty of spare wool, and gloves and helmets. All should have torches, and the leader may well take a head torch, so as to have both hands free. Besides their own axes, a short auxiliary axe can be of great use, to make footing for the leader on stiff pitches.

Snow and Ice Surfaces

These will include deep, dry, powdery snow, frequently with a light, breakable crust, good hard snow so hard and tough that steps must be cut in it with the ice-axe, and finally, the hard, brittle 100 per cent. ice encountered on steep pitches in rocky gullies.

Weather dictates which it shall be, for new fallen snow may be slowly or quickly transformed to hard snow by the alternating action of frost and thaw and also by wind. A sudden thaw may make the snow risky, especially if it softens the top layer where it is resting on a steep slope of hard frozen snow or ice. Experience is needed to judge of this.

As to season snow may fall and lie for a time on the north-east face of Ben Nevis in late September. The greatest accumulation is usually found from February to April, but difficult snow and ice work may be encountered as late as May. A snow glissade (slide) of 500 feet may even be found as late as the end of June.

FIG. 38—KICKING STEPS UPHILL

Conditions vary with the different years. The onset of a warm south-west wind may thaw the snow very quickly, and a gully climb which is safe, though difficult, under frost may, in a few hours, become dangerous owing to avalanches or to the fall of cornices from the top of the gully. Ice or stones may fall from the rocky walls at the same time.

It is unusual to find an open snow-slope at as great an

angle to the horizontal as 45 degrees. With good nailed boots you can easily walk up a 30 degrees slope. Slopes over 50 degrees will only be found in gullies. Here, they are often broken up by protruding rocks or ice pitches. For short distances you can climb ice pitches by cutting with the axe both footholds and handholds, even though the slope is as much as 70 degrees; but the work is severe and progress is slow.

If you climb rock ridges in winter, you often find a glazing of ice on the rocks; this is known as *verglas*, and is due to rain or mist freezing on the rocks.

At the tops of gullies, especially in late winter, there are often great eaves of overhanging snow called cornices. These may be difficult or even impossible to surmount. In thaw conditions, also, portions will break away and fall down the gully. In late spring this is bound to occur and you must look out for it. At this season, too, the retreating and melting snowbeds lying against steep rocks leave gaps, fissures, caverns and tunnels. These deep holes, often with very thin roofs, like the *bergschrunds* of the Alps, may be dangerous traps.

Use of the Ice-Axe in Ascending

Your early practice should be on easy slopes or gullies without any ice pitches, and without any cornices above. You can climb moderate slopes by kicking steps and using the axe spike as a steady or anchor if needed. As the angle steepens, the snow will probably give place to hard snow and the leader will have to cut steps. At first a single stroke with the adze end will slash out a secure step. At intervals on a long slope it is advisable to cut three or four larger steps for bringing up the weaker members of the party. On steep slopes, of course, only one member may be moving at a time.

For belaying the leader gets slightly above his axe, and uses his full weight to thrust it into the snow as far as possible. The rope is placed round the axe shaft at snow level, and the leader stands level with the rope. The snow friction lessens the strain on the axe.

In really tough snow or snow-ice steps are difficult to cut and many blows may be required. The step should always be made so as to slope slightly inwards. In cutting steps you should stand upright, in balance, grip the shaft with

FIG. 39—CUTTING STEPS UPHILL

both hands if you can, swing it no higher than your head, preserve rhythm in your strokes and, as far as possible, let the weight of the axe do the work. The shaft is oval, so that you can hold the axe lightly except at the instant of impact. This will save energy. Learn to balance safely on one foot. If the slope is both long and steep you may find it better to cut a zig-zag ladder, with an extra big step at each turn. The reasons for the zig-zag are that the cutting position is easier than upon a vertical ladder; it is easier to rest at times, it is easier for a novice to ascend a zig-zag, and it is very much easier to descend if necessary during a retreat. When resting you should use the axe spike as a strut against the slope and not use the pick to hang on by. The safest position is upright, because that keeps the feet firm in the steps, and your only risk comes from their slipping.

FIG. 40—CUTTING STEPS ACROSS A SLOPE

The steps should never be too far apart for the convenience of the shortest man and close steps are easier to descend should you have to return. If the surface layer is crust with powder snow underneath or insecure wet snow, then, although it may be quicker to kick steps in the crust, there is risk of the top layer sliding off altogether and sweeping the party with it; so safety demands that you should remove the top layer and cut steps in the underlying hard snow or ice. Dry powder snow may also cascade in gullies during frosty weather, but this is seldom dangerous and you can usually dodge it.

Short, steep pitches of real ice demand more carefully fashioned steps and may take a long time to negotiate. Two members of the party should come up to the foot of such an ice pitch to belay the leader, and use two ice-axes driven well into the snow and sloped slightly uphill.

FIG. 41—BELAYING ON ICE

Neither of these two should be also on the ice. The rope to the leader should not be twisted round the axe; it should be run behind it at snow level, paid out carefully and held and watched all the time. If the leader then "comes off" the strain will come on second and third as one man. On such a pitch the leader should cut steps directly upwards, for each step will have to serve first as handhold, then as foothold. In a party of three the novice should come last, so that the leader can concentrate on his own job.

On such climbing an auxiliary short axe as described in Chapter 2 for the leader to use as a step is safer than to use combined tactics (e.g., a shoulder from the second). One such extra axe is enough in a party. You should never use combined tactics unless it is reasonably certain that the route will "go" above the difficulty. The leader's rucksack

FIG. 42—BELAYING ON SNOW

may have to be hauled up on a separate rope. The leader should not bring up his second until he is well above the ice himself or can anchor himself securely on good snow or on rock.

There may always be a final barrier at the top of a gully, in the form of a cornice of hard snow. On Ben Nevis cornices may be as much as 40 feet thick. Although overhanging you can usually tackle them where they are at their lowest, where they are only vertical, or where a break-away has lowered and retracted the lip. There is often a hollow running along below the cornice, and to this the leader should bring up the rest of the party, so that they may belay themselves and safeguard him while he advances. Here again the leader may have to borrow an extra ice-axe to drive horizontally into the snow wall as hand- and foothold; the short auxiliary axe will do this well. Finally he will crawl over the top, go well back from the edge and secure the others while ascending. Cornices have been tunnelled through on occasion. In thaw weather when cornices may always break away in part, the gullies below them should be avoided.

The Ice-Axe in Descent

Climbing down either rocks or snow and ice is a necessary and badly neglected part of the training of every complete mountaineer. Sometimes a descending retreat is forced on a party in order to avoid a wintry night out; so it is better to acquire the necessary experience, preferably down an easy snow gully already made familiar by a former climb. If a ready-made set of steps is available the job is easy. The leader goes last man on the rope, a good second man leads downwards and the weaker members go between. If steps must be cut, good balance is needed here even more than on the ascent; it may be necessary to cut with one hand—very tiring work if the snow is hard. When moving down, hold the axe by the shaft as a steady against the slope behind; move deliberately and keep always an upright position. A zig-zag course is easier to cut downhill, and for weaker members of the party to come down. Even on slopes where you could ascend by kicking, a slash with the adze is advisable to make a safe descent. If time is very limited, you can make secure by all the party hooking the picks of their axes into the snow and descending carefully sideways. The rope should be kept fairly taut. Progress in such fashion may be slow but it will be continuous. Remember that hard-frozen slopes should on no account be glissaded, if at all steep. Roping down an ice-pitch (on the doubled rope) is done in the same way as

PLATE 1 The Yukon pack frame. This is a good way of carrying large or awkwardly shaped loads.

PLATE 2
SCOTLAND,
Glencoe: The Red Slab Route on the Rannoch Wall of the Buchaille Etive Mor. This photograph illustrates the use of the running belay for protecting the leader.

PLATE 3
SCOTLAND,
Glencoe: Early morning shadows above the lonely cottage at Loch Achtriochtan with the cliffs of Stob Coire nam Beith rising above.

A. C. D. Small

E. *Webster*

PLATE 4
SCOTLAND:
The Cairngorms from Glenmore Lodge. These hills form the largest area of land in this island over 4,000 ft. and snow lingers on them almost to July.

PLATE 5
SCOTLAND :
Cairn Toul from
Braeriach.

Mrs. J. E. Brush

G. A. R. Spence

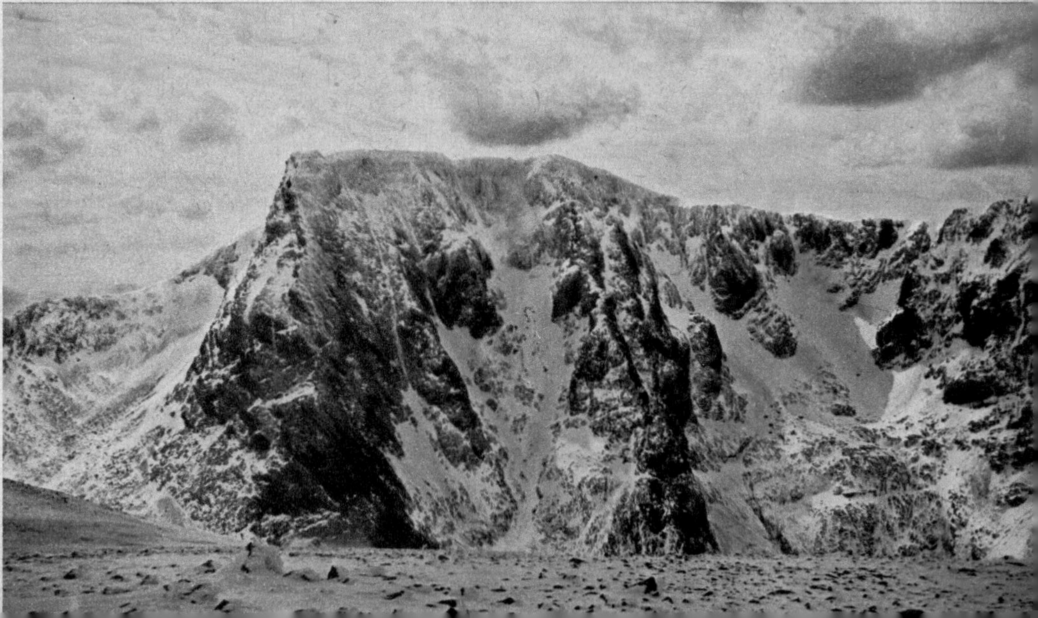

PLATE 6
SCOTLAND :
The cliffs of Ben Nevis from across the Mhuillin Glen. In winter conditions such as this, Ben Nevis presents climbing problems as severe or more severe than any usually encountered in the Alps, with the additional handicap of limited daylight.

PLATE 7 ROSS-SHIRE: Ben More Coigach. Stac Polly is seen between the cliffs of Sgurr an Fhidleir and Sgorr Deas, the tops of Ben More Coigach.

PLATE 8 LAKE DISTRICT : Oliverson's on Gimmer Crag.

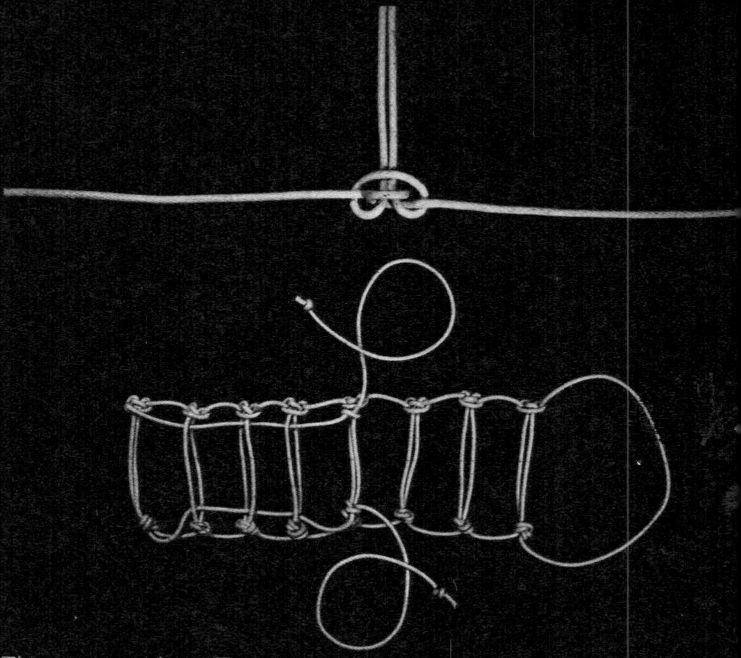

The rope stretcher Type A

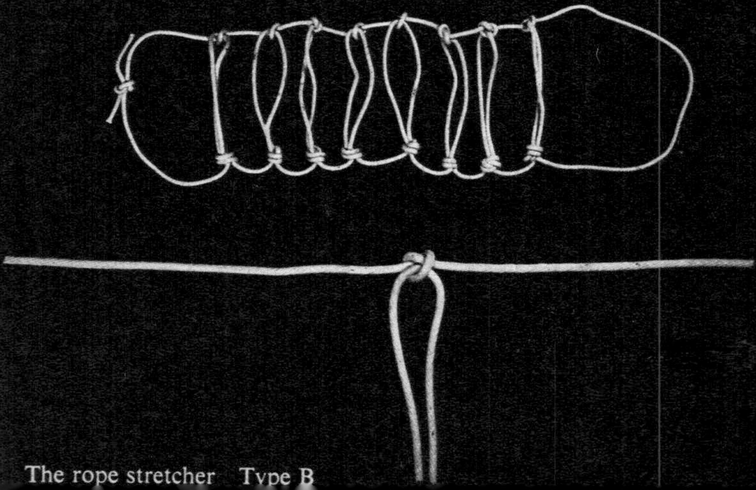

The rope stretcher Type B

G. A. Dummett

PLATE 9 NORTH WALES : Crib Goch Pinnacle. The route goes up the edge of the buttress.

PLATE 10 NORTH WALES : A training ground for beginners and the most popular mountain in the district—Tryfan.

PLATE 11 NORTH WALES : Dinas Cromlech. This cliff provides a number of routes of medium length and of high quality.

PLATE 12 NORTH WALES: The Crackstone Rib on Carreg Wastad—a grade IV rockclimb.

PLATE 13
NORTH WALES
Lliwedd: The "swing" pitch on the Garter Traverse. This cliff gives a large number of routes of a high standard of difficulty and interest.

PLATE 14
NORTH WALES
The East Buttress of Clogwyn du'r Arddu. The climbs here are among the hardest in the country.

PLATE 15
NORTH WALES
Clogwyn y Grochan—a nursery for 'tigers.'

PLATE 16
NORTH WALES
Clogwyn du'r Arddu.

PLATE 17
NORTH WALES
Tryfan and the Ogwen Valley in winter.

G. A. Dummett

PLATE 18
NORTH WALES
Cwm Idwal — a school for rock-climbing.

FIG. 43—CUTTING STEPS DOWNHILL

FIG. 44—KICKING STEPS DOWNHILL

for rock climbing. If the party has got into severe difficulties and night approaches it may be necessary to sacrifice an ice-axe as an anchor. The last man in this case should be very careful when he takes off.

Snow and Ice on Rocks and Ridges

Snow may mask and make easier pitches in gullies; but it will generally make ridge and buttress climbs much more difficult. If a narrow ridge is corniced two methods can be tried. Flog down the snow and climb the uncovered rock, or traverse along the flanking snow wall well back from the edge, or even traverse below the ridge. The overhang of a cornice is not always easy to judge, so to pass it safely may cost you time and labour. Cornices on both sides of a ridge are unusual in Britain. Steep ridges and buttresses under snow offer many problems. Even in spring, in shaded places, there may be a thin veneer of verglas on the rocks. If this is only on some of the ledges and not general it is not so bad; in some other cases the ice can be chipped off the rock, but if the glaze is thin and the condition is general then the climb should be abandoned.

You must learn to climb moderately difficult rocks with the ice-axe in your hand and not on a sling. The axe is often very useful as a steadying prop, especially during the descent. On more difficult rocks you must make sure it is well secured, without danger to persons below.

On steep ridges you may sometimes be unable to climb wall-like steps straight up the crest. The snow then encountered while traversing the flank of the ridge below the crest is often insecure, especially where the underlying rock structure slopes like a roof. Such a passage will test the leader. Belays will be few, but he can perhaps wedge the axe pick into a crack in the rock or between rock and ice and so protect his snow steps. You can often hack out a good step in frozen turf and obtain a good hitch. On all such passages an upright stance is the safest.

Near the 4,000 foot level on such mountains as Ben Nevis the rocks are often thickly encased in masses of frost crystals growing out into the direction of the wind. This may give you severe and icy conditions calling for hours of laborious step cutting; and you should make an extra allowance of time for the possibility. On the other hand late winter snow lying at a steep angle on the flank of a steep ridge can be more secure in Britain than summer snow at the same angle in the Alps. Always test such snow, for its security depends on the structure of the rock below it. Powder snow in early winter is not very trustworthy.

Avalanches

Small avalanches occur in Britain, especially during thaw weather and in narrow, steep gullies. Sooner or later the cornices formed above gullies must break away and fall down the gully to consolidate below in big rounded masses. Dry snow avalanches during frost are less dangerous, and small masses of powder snow often come down gullies in windy, frosty weather after a new snowfall. A sudden thaw after a heavy snowfall may make it risky to glissade down steep open snow slopes. There is no sure way of telling whether snow in gullies will avalanche or not. Throwing a stone on to the snow is inconclusive, though it may indicate at once that the snow is in a highly dangerous condition. On a descent an experienced leader, belayed from above, should go down and decide for himself if the gully is safe—and he should err on the side of caution. On an ascent in reasonably good weather there should be little danger if the steps are made into firm snow beneath the surface layer—and if every tendency to slip is at once checked.

Glissading

This is best learned on the lower hills in spring. Uneven snow and a boulder-strewn surface are useless. The standing glissade is the safer and more useful method, and somewhat resembles ski running. You should be almost erect and in balance. The ice-axe is not a prop for you to lean upon; it is a rudder and an emergency brake, auxiliary to the action of your feet. Pace is regulated by the feet, by driving in the heels to check, or by pointing the toes downward to accelerate. One foot has a slight lead and carries the weight; the other follows slightly to one side, but not straddled out; a wide foot base with the weight

FIG. 45—GLISSADING

on both feet makes only for poor balance and cannot withstand any jerk due to varying surfaces or gradient. The front leg is nearly straight when running fast, the other comes up and passes it if you want to change direction. Over furrowed snow you should lean back somewhat and steady with the axe. Roped glissades are not very satisfactory, especially with more than two persons. There should be no glissading if the slope cannot be seen to run out gently at the bottom, or if there is any avalanche danger or if it looks as if the slope changes to hard, icy snow such as in a former avalanche slide.

For a dangerous instance to avoid—the funnel on an open hillside which leads to the top of a gully may look to be good glissading snow; but the snow in the gully will probably be ice, where the glissade would become uncontrollable.

A sitting glissade may be feasible where the snow is not good enough for standing, as happens in late spring. Control sitting is not so easy as standing. If the snow piles up under you, side roll and get clear. Never use the pick as a brake in these circumstances. Grip the shaft near the head and a little lower down with the other hand, and press the spike backwards into the snow under your shoulder or to either side as may be necessary to brake or steer. By arching the body upward between the heels and the axe thrust, full brake power is developed.

If, owing to an unexpected change in the surface to frozen hard snow or ice, control of the glissade is lost, it may perhaps be regained or at least the speed of the fall reduced by another method of braking. This is shown in the illustration (46). It is important that the spike of the ice-axe should not be pressed too abruptly into the ice, if so the axe will be wrenched from your grip; the pressure must be applied gradually until control is regained.

It may be expedient to glissade some gullies one at a time in pitches with a long rope, even if there are one or two short steep bits. But even so control must never be lost by the moving man and the gully must be known to the leader. Remember the possibility of there being a short pitch or a miniature chasm (*bergschrund*) near the bottom, and be careful of a run-out on to snow-hidden boulders. Note too that any part of a gully exposed to the sun may run a good deal faster than the rest.

The more arduous the winter expedition in prospect, the more vital it is to plot it out beforehand, with a full study of the weather, the snow conditions, the valley approaches and the time needed for each stage. There must be no late start, and no racing or minute-losing during the ascent. Only in this way can you be sure of a good reserve of physical energy and mental tone, should the final stages of a

FIG. 46—BRAKING ON HARD SNOW OR ICE

long contest prove stormy, dark or exhausting. In fact all the general rules given in chapter 3 must be followed with much greater care than is necessary in the long and warm days of summer.

Chapter 7

MOUNTAIN CAMPING

THIS chapter deals only with camping in the British hills in spring, summer and autumn. Winter camping is highly specialised and demands arctic equipment, and is consequently the sport of the few.

Further, certain assumptions are made. First that you are camping primarily to climb and second that you have already some general camping experience. If not, the more general technique is given in the handbook of the Camping Club of Great Britain and in such books as *Camping and Woodcraft* by Kephart.

Camping in mountains involves certain hardships. In compensation for these you will be camping high and much nearer your climbs, and in a high camp the climber will both find himself closer to the mountain in spirit and he will also be broadening his experience of mountain craft and of mountain ways. The beauty of the inner sanctuaries of hills at dawn and dusk, and the silence among hills at night are secrets unknown to the valley and hotel-bound climber.

The Camp Site

The first step is to choose a suitable place to camp. This should be dry and not liable to flood in any circumstances. Hollows and ground adjacent to watercourses should be avoided as the level of water in mountain streams can rise extremely rapidly. If you are choosing a site in dry weather you should also avoid places showing evidence of former flooding. You will usually find it difficult to find level sites, but only a very uncomfortable camp can be pitched on a steep hillside, and if the camp is to be maintained for long it may even be worth while building a level platform of rocks and turf as a foundation for the floor of the tent. In general it is not sound to pitch a tent at a good view-point, since this rarely gives the wind-shelter which you will need in a gale. For a few days camping it is worth while building a wall of boulders on the side from which the prevailing wind comes. If there is not good holding ground for the tent pegs the guys should be secured to boulders and you should take care that the guys do not chafe anywhere. Take plenty of spare guyline and pegs of the " Bulldog " type. On some fellsides you may have to dig drainage channels to divert the surface water from flowing over the groundsheet. In short, in choosing and preparing the site you must guard against the worst imaginable conditions—sooner or later they will arrive.

In bad weather, especially on sites remote from shelter, do not be pigheaded about maintaining the camp. If the evacuation route is over difficult ground it is more sensible to beat a retreat in time rather than to risk having to abandon your gear.

The site should be near a supply of good water for drinking, washing and washing up. There is not often any difficulty about this in Britain—one of your chief difficulties is to avoid having too much water in the camp. A stream is to be preferred to a lake, but it is quite pleasant to be near a lake also so as to get the bathing.

Insects

The Scottish midge in season—June to September inclusive—must be experienced to be believed, and it makes camping impossible unless the utmost precautions are taken. Avoid marshy ground and a too sheltered site; a breeze affords excellent protection. Face and neck can be protected by a fine netting bag well tucked into the coat collar; this should be dyed green as white attracts midges. Exclude them from the tent by a completely sewn-in groundsheet and by closing the door and ventilators with very fine mesh netting, dyed green, which can be lifted for entrance. This should ensure comfortable sleeping quarters as any intruders tend to congregate at the top of the tent. Before rising, midges can be stupefied by tobacco smoke or more effectively by a special Chinese incense sold for the purpose. A smoking Primus will do but is unpleasant. Anti-midge preparations, such as citronella oil, have only transient effect if any. In calm weather cooking will almost certainly have to be done inside the tent and meals taken there.

Lighting

The two most simple and reliable methods are the candle and the electric torch. The former requires some gadget to fix it to the tent pole or it may be stuck on an unopened food tin. A torch should always be taken for emergency use. The best illumination of all is given by an incandescent mantle fitted on your primus stove.

Clothes Drying

This is one of the most difficult problems for the camper. Much can be done, with lavish expenditure of fuel and some sacrifice of comfort, by hanging things up in the tent and keeping the stove going. On returning to camp after a wet day, strip completely, rub down and change into dry clothes kept with the bedding inside the main rucksack. Damp clothes can be put on again next morning without ill effect. However, climbing from a camp cannot usually be continued for more than about three or four days in bad weather.

Bivouacing

For light short duration camps a tent is not always necessary, a sleeping bag with a waterproof cover is sufficient. In this way it is possible to keep the total weight of equipment light enough to make it not too laborious to carry it uphill for long distances. Unless two sleeping bags one inside the other are used it is not possible to keep completely dry in wet weather, as condensation from one's own sweat will make the sleeping bag damp. It is therefore not practicable to maintain a comfortable tentless bivouac in wet weather, since you will always get wet while making or breaking camp, unless there is a convenient cave or hollow sheltered by a boulder nearby in which you can cook, eat and change. However, in fine weather your intimacy with the hills and the sky which is the greatest virtue of hill camping is further enhanced by the absence of even canvas shutting them out.

Chapter 8

MOUNTAIN RESCUE AND FIRST AID

IT is difficult to give advice and instruction that will apply to all accidents in the mountains—except the truism that the good climber should not have them. Objective dangers are rare in British hills and mishaps are usually due to over-ambition, or lack of care, or ignorance of elementary principles. Unfortunately, everyone is capable of making mistakes, not only the beginner but the expert as well, and this book will have served a useful purpose if it helps in reducing the number of accidents due to ignorance.

Sooner or later nearly everyone who walks or climbs in British hills will be confronted with an accident with which he or she will have to deal, just as nearly everyone who uses the roads will also be so confronted. In the latter case, however, professional help can be obtained very quickly, but in the mountains the difficulties of movement may cause a delay of many hours between the time of the accident and the arrival of the victim in hospital. This delay is quite often a most serious factor, and it is every climber's duty to know how to minimize its effects.

Mountain Accidents

Let us then assume that an accident has happened and that the scene is in the mountains.

The first thing to be done is to make the victim as warm and comfortable as possible, because this will reduce shock. His body should be insulated from the cold mountain by heather, bracken and a mackintosh or coat. If he has to be left while help is sought he should be tied to an anchor, even if he is unconscious. Someone should be left with him if there are more than two in the party, because the effect of loneliness on an injured man, especially on returning from an unconscious state, will be to increase shock. It is the leader's duty then to the rest of the party, if they cannot help further, to get them on to safe ground, that is ground on which they can safely and competently return to the valley on their own. If access to the scene of the accident is difficult a fixed rope should be left to assist the rescuers ; but not at the expense of the safety of the rest of the party. If anyone needs lowering to safety the triple bowline is the best knot to use. This is made by tying an ordinary bowline in a rope doubled for three or four yards. One of the resulting loops is used for each leg and the central one for the waist. The loops should not be too tight; a hammock-like suspension is required.

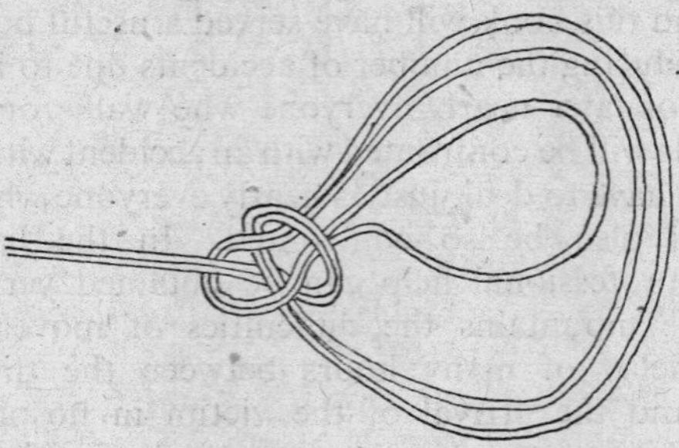

FIG. 47—THE TRIPLE BOWLINE

First Aid Posts

A list of first aid posts is given in Appendix III. If one of these is within reach help should be summoned from there, preferably from one with a supervisor, because this will save time, trouble and anxiety. If the nearest one is fairly distant the telephone should be used, but if help has to be summoned from more than one valley, requests for doctor and ambulance should not be duplicated. Such places as Craig yr Ysfa, or Clogwyn Du'r-arddu are cases in point. Helpers may be needed from both the Ogwen and Llanberis valleys, but ambulance and doctor should only be called from one.

In remote areas, or if exposure is likely to be long or serious, every effort should be made to get the patient to shelter until a rescue party can be gathered. For cases of exhaustion or minor accidents, the rope stretcher described below can be used for this purpose. If the injuries are too serious for the patient to be moved without a rigid stretcher, or further help, a wind shield, or shelter, should be built round him and every means used to keep him warm.

The Messenger

The messenger sent for help should travel swiftly and safely. If his services are not needed after delivery of the message, he might well be spared the labour of returning with the rescue party. He should carry a written message giving the time and place of the accident, the nature of the injuries, and any further information that may help the rescue party. Money will be required, too, if a telephone has to be used.

Organization

A leader, and a pathfinder should be appointed. Confusion is apt to occur, especially in the dark, with helpers coming from different places. It is therefore better to arrange a rendezvous and for someone to keep in touch with and to direct supporting parties. Relief measures should be organized at the base.

Helpers

Helpers can usually be recruited from other climbers or walkers in the district. At least four stretcher bearers are required, six are better; and for long carries a relay of four more will be necessary. Sometimes shepherds or quarrymen may have to be called upon to help. They have always responded generously to these calls and they should be compensated for their services. The continuance of just and friendly relations with them is so important that the First Aid Committee will advance the money to pay suitable recompense, although the cost would be considered to be the responsibility of the patient, his friends, or, failing them, his Club or Association, and the Committee expect that any payment it may make will be refunded. Payment should bear some relation to the work done and be made on the recommendation of the supervisor or some other responsible person; a maximum sum of £1 for each helper is suggested. The services of a doctor and ambulance should be paid for and the cost of meals for the rescuers, and of replacements or repair of damage to first aid apparatus.

The First Aid Committee will always use its influence to alleviate any genuine case of hardship incurred in rescue service, but it cannot accept any financial responsibility other than the provision of equipment in the first instance.

Checking the Kit

The re-assembly, drying and cleaning of the equipment is important. The suffering of another may be prolonged, or even a life lost, if the kit is not in good order and ready for the next call. Deficiencies or damage should be reported to the supervisor, or to the Hon. Secretary of the First Aid Committee of Mountaineering Clubs, A. S. Pigott, Hill House, Cheadle Hulme, Stockport.

The Press

Relatives of the injured should be informed, and it is better to give a considered factual acount of the accident to reporters rather than let them gather information from casual sources, which may result in a distorted version being published and cause unnecessary pain and distress.

Search Parties

Another problem which faces responsible mountaineers is the determination of the right time to go out and look for an overdue member, or party. There is no easy answer to this problem, but it can be made easier if everyone before leaving the hut or hotel in the morning leaves a note of where he is going and when he intends to return, and a log book might be kept for this purpose. This will save many fruitless searches; nothing is more exasperating for a party of would-be rescuers, after spending a wet and laborious night on the hills, then to discover, when they return weary in the morning, that the people they set out to find had spent a comfortable night in the next valley and intended to do so when they set out. If plans are changed during the course of the day, as they often are, it is incumbent on the party to let their hut, or hotel companions know of the change, either by a 'phone message or a note.

If a party is seriously overdue—say more than three hours—the question of a search party has to be faced. In the case of rock climbers it is a fairly simple matter, if the cliff they have been climbing on is known, and in rock climbing centres there will usually be a number of people who are competent to go up in the dark and find out what has happened, and then to take whatever action is necessary. If the party that is missing is walking, or is climbing and has not said where, the difficulty is much increased and action will depend on circumstances. If there is a bright moon and an effective search party can be organized it can set out at once—though British hills usually save up particularly dark and stormy nights for these occasions. To set out in such circumstances demands an experienced party with good local knowledge: a large party of inexperienced people is useless and may result in further accidents. It is sometimes better in such cases to make arrangements deliberately so that the search can start on the hills at the crack of dawn. With a few hours sleep everyone will be better at the job, and the organizer can make certain that the search is properly planned, and that it starts off properly equipped. Any delay after first light is inexcusable; the party must be absolutely ready at that time on the nearest road or track to the area to be searched. The help of a shepherd and his dogs can be most valuable.

Distress Signal

The alpine distress signal can be used when it is necessary to attract the attention of another party in an emergency. It must never be used for any other purpose. It can be given by lamp, voice, whistle or flag, and consists of six blasts or flashes in a minute followed by a minute's silence and a repeat six blasts and should be repeated until attention is attracted. The acknowledgment, or "O.K." signal consists of three blasts in a minute followed by a minute's silence, and repeat.

FIRST AID

The principles to be observed by those rendering First Aid are:—

1. The stopping of bleeding and sterilizing of open wounds.
2. The immobilizing of broken limbs so that movement does not cause the slightest pain.
3. The reduction of shock by removing pain and applying warmth.

It is not possible to lay down precise rules to cover a wide variety of circumstances, but, in general, little else should be attempted, and what can be postponed is better left to the skilled attention and aseptic conditions that a hospital affords. It is strongly recommended that, if a patient is, or can be made, fit to travel, he should be sent to a large general hospital, even a distant one, where he can receive the advantages of specialized attention and equipment pending recovery, which may take months.

PAIN. If in pain inject one ampoule (*see below*). If pain is present an hour later, inject another. In a long carry, if the patient is warm and pain still present, inject a third ampoule one and a half hours before the valley is reached. (If under twelve years inject only one-half ampoule.) Inject under pinched-up skin on the outer surface of the arm, after cleaning with spirit, if available.

Do not give morphia or brandy in cases of severe head injury.

WOUNDS. Clean with spirit, and dust or spray with sulphanilamide powder. (The type of antiseptic is liable to change with modern practice.) Apply Shell dressing or gauze and elastoplast (best), or wool and bandage. Do not *plug* non-bleeding wounds. Do not stitch wounds; draw the edges together with plaster over gauze. If the wounds are dirty or extensive give two tablets of M. & B. 760 every two hours.

HÆMORRHAGE. Do not give stimulants. Inject contents of ampoule.

If bleeding continues in a limb after bandaging tightly, and if it is really serious, it is permissible to stop it by tying a scarf, or even rope, round the limb with underlying cloth or other padding for protection. This tourniquet must be invariably released one half-hour later. It can be re-applied. Bleeding has never yet required this serious treatment in a climbing accident.

FRACTURES. Every broken limb must be immobilized by fixation to splints, the body or the stretcher, so that movement is possible without pain. Transport must not be continued if the movement causes pain.

Broken Limbs

ARM. Angular splint on inside. Straight splint or pieces of wood all round. Place jersey, cloth or cotton-wool between the skin and the splints. Bandage from shoulder to wrist; and fix the whole tightly to the chest.

COLLAR-BONE. Place hand near opposite collar-bone and bind the whole shoulder and limb to the chest.

LEG. Insert boot through the circle of the Thomas iron leg-splint (short iron on the inside). Pass the leg down until he is apparently sitting on the ring. Fasten firmly by the attached gaiter, or rope loops, to the boot;

then pass climbing rope through the gaiter strap, or rope loops, and pull ruthlessly on the boot to make the leg immobile within the iron splint by fastening the rope to the bottom end of the splint under extreme tension; it will slacken later. Then pass a bandage of puttees, scarves, or rope round the leg and splint from the top to the bottom so that the whole is one solid piece and can be moved roughly without causing pain.

SPINE. With the slightest suspicion of a fractured spine roll him very gently on to his face and lift slowly on to the stretcher, roping him securely to it. The boot toes should be pointing downwards over the lower end of the canvas. The spine should always be uppermost, but the shoulders, arms and head should be made comfortable by cushioning.

Any movement, even rolling on to the abdomen is bad. A doctor present can change these instructions; even then move the injured climber like a piece of precious cracked china which must not be broken.

SUMMARY. Warmth and freedom from pain are far more important than speed. If movement causes pain, first try roping him more tightly to his splints or stretcher. If unsuccessful, give him a second morphia ampoule. Hot, concentrated sugar drinks are the best food; alcohol is bad.

After use of the tubonic ampoule syringes **it is of the utmost importance that full details, stating date, place and name of person on whom used, be sent immediately to:**

Wilson H. Hey, F.R.C.S.,
16, St. John Street,
Manchester, 3.

It is requested that, after an accident, a brief report, including name and address of patient, his Club or Association, and particulars of any replacements required, be sent to:

A. S. Pigott,
Hill House,
Cheadle Hulme,
Stockport.
(Tel.: Cheadle Hulme 257)

Equipment

The standard mountain first aid equipment is listed below. Equipments of this type are kept in the principal mountain centres in Great Britain. Details are given of these centres in Appendix III.

The outfit consists of a stretcher and two rucksacks of medical and warmth supplies with directions for first aid.

Before the base is left STIMULANTS, FOOD, SUGAR (if not in rucksacks) AND HOT DRINKS SHOULD BE ADDED. PLENTY OF ROPE MUST BE TAKEN. TAKE BOTH RUCKSACKS.

RUCKSACK NO. 1 contains:

List of contents and instructions.

1 eiderdown bag (or blankets) with detachable waterproof cover and tie tapes.

1 Balaclava Helmet.

1 iron Thomas leg-splint with spat for attachment to boot; to be kept tied to rucksack.

1 case for medical appliances, containing :—
6 Demette bandages, 6 ins.; 6 triangular bandages; 1 roll 1-in. 10-yds. adhesive plaster; 4 rolls 3-in. 1-yd. Elastoplast bandage; ball of string or tape; 2 straight arm splints; 1 angular arm splint; Antiseptic (M. & B.) Powder Dredger; iodine; 2 shell dressings; gauze; cotton wool; scissors; safety pins; 1 pair 5-ins. dressing forceps; 1 pair Spencer Wells clamp forceps; linen thread (No. 60); 2 needles (straight surgical 2½").

2 TUBONIC AMPOULE Syringes each containing ⅓rd. grain OMNOPON (Morphia) in solution ready for injection.

Cube sugar in jar.

RUCKSACK NO. 2 contains:—

Folding Glacier Lantern.
6 Candles.
2 Kettles.
3 Hot Water bottles.

3 Cups (2 drinking and 1 feeding cup).
1 Monitor stove to be kept filled with paraffin.
Meta fuel.
Spare jet and jet key.
Small spoon.
Jug.
2 Thermos flasks.

THE THOMAS STRETCHER. The Thomas stretcher has a frame of duralumin tubing and has extending handles; it is made to be kept and carried assembled. The later models have wooden runners. It can be lowered down rock, grass, heather or scree and will stand ordinary rough usage, but it must be remembered that undue vigour in dragging and a boulder-strewn slope will wreck anything, and that it is designed as a light-weight carrying stretcher.

Place eiderdown on the waterproof cover (or blanket) opened out on the stretcher. The double thigh support, if included, should be placed on top of the eiderdown and care taken to see that it is securely fastened to the cross-bar by its leather hinge. Adjust patient in splint. Apply hot water bottles. Wrap cover overall and secure with the four straps provided. If the single Thomas iron leg-splint is used the bottom should be tied or strapped to crossbar. Support may also be needed at feet, fork and armpits if lowering vertically. Tie the lowering rope to the top crossbar. Test comfort before beginning to lower. No weight on injured limbs. Make a sling for an uninjured leg to take part of the weight. Extending handles allow view of feet to carriers who will find it easier to walk downhill with the stretcher held sideways between them. Put the head through the yoke straps, which then distribute the weight. Keep the stretcher as level as possible. Extra helpers can steady and take part of the weight by the side straps.

THE DUFF STRETCHER. The Duff stretcher has a frame of steel tubing and is made to be lowered or slid down rock and mountain slopes. It is laterally collapsible and in preparing the stretcher it is best to fix the central hinge and head-end strut first, locking these in position by inserting the foot-end cross bar through its hole in the pole, where it is secured by a small locking catch underneath.

With the stretcher there is a spring leaf undercarriage with hooked clamps at either end, which, when screwed tight, grip the runners. Black marks on the runners indicate the centre of gravity. With the single wheel pinned into the central socket the weight of the patient will be taken from the bearer's arms. In high wind or rain the stretcher may be carried to an accident folded, but it will often be found easier to take it with the wheel in position as its own vehicle and carrying on it rucksacks, blankets, Thomas iron leg splint and other gear.

The patient, warmly wrapped, will be fastened on the stretcher with the body-belt provided. If he must be lowered vertically the perineal strap will be brought forward below the crotch and buckled, one on either side, to the front of the body-belt. If the Thomas iron leg-splint is used, fix its lower end in the clips of the crossbar. When lowering or sliding down slopes the leader can guide the stretcher with strap fixed to crossbar and two helpers behind will tie their slings to after corners and pull or check as required. On reaching level ground, or a path, the undercarriage and wheel (always to be carried on the stretcher itself—wheel under pillow and undercarriage in pocket of body-belt) will be fastened in place for more rapid progress. One bearer in front and two on either side behind will be able to watch their steps. They must all keep firm hold of the stretcher.

THE PIGOTT STRETCHER. The illustrations (Plates, Type A and Type B) shew two methods of making a stretcher easily and quickly from a climbing rope. The difference lies only in the knot used to secure the loops to one of the longitudinal ropes. This form of stretcher is useful for carrying the victims of minor accident or exhaustion to warmth and shelter in the shortest possible time, but it is laborious to carry, usually uncomfortable for the patient, and better equipment should always be sought and sent to meet the carrying party. Cases of serious injury require a rigid stretcher. It is repeated that broken limbs must be immobilized so that movement does not cause pain. A broken leg might be tied firmly to the sound one; a broken arm to the chest.

The knot in Type A is a better job and should be used if the rope is eighty feet or more. Type B requires less rope and may be used if the rope is a short one. In both types the loops, which are tied with a simple overhand knot, begin eighteen feet from one end of the rope and are tied at eight or nine inch intervals. With Type A they should be about three feet long *before* tying and a convenient measurement is to take the distance between one's mouth and outstretched finger tips. Type B needs loops of only thirty inches *before* tying, the distance from mouth to base of palm. In both cases they should be about twenty-three inches long in their final state after the free rope has been passed through and attached.

Before securing the first loop allow for enough rope to pass over the shoulder of the end bearer. If there are only four bearers it will be necessary to make a shoulder loop at both ends even if it means shortening the stretcher, and it is really easier to carry with two such loops; the front bearer pulls forward, the rear man resists the pull and the longitudinal ropes are thus kept more taut. Other helpers take their place and lift at the sides. A disadvantage is that the front bearer is apt to bump against the patient's feet and in the case of a foot or leg injury it is better at that end to have two bearers, one on each side. This means a minimum of five bearers, but more are desirable; they tire quickly, particularly those at the sides by the patient's hips. If the rope is a long one the extra length can usefully be employed by threading the two ends back to the centre and using them as carrying slings as shown on the photograph.

The bed of the stretcher can be padded and the patient wrapped and covered with coats, sweaters and so on, but care should be taken to tuck loose ends well in to prevent them trailing on the ground. A pillow can be improvised from a rucksack.

Chapter 9

WHERE TO WALK AND CLIMB

THE most satisfactory way of choosing a district to walk in is probably to look at a comparatively small scale relief map of Great Britain and select any district which appeals where the contours rise over 1,000 or 1,500 feet. and then to buy the 1″ O.S. or Bartholomew map of the district and start planning where to walk. In this way you are likely to light upon some part of the hill lands of Britain which you would otherwise never visit and having walked over it learn to love it.

The choice for rock climbing is more restricted. Geological chance has determined where the cliffs shall be, and they are not necessarily associated with all high ground.

Southern England

There is a desperate scarcity of good rock in southern England. Near Tunbridge Wells in Kent there are a number of outcrops of sandstone from 20 to 40 feet high, which provide problem climbs of high technical interest and difficulty and which are very popular with climbers condemned to live in London. There are also the rotten limestone cliffs of Cheddar Gorge; which can hardly be recommended although climbs have been done on them. And there is the wholly good granite of the Cornish sea-cliffs. For these last it is advisable to be a strong swimmer as well as a climber.

Midlands and North Midlands

In the Midlands and the north Midlands there are a large number of rock outcrops, of sandstone, limestone or grit-stone, of varied sizes some being very worthy cliffs. These are too numerous to deal with in detail here and the local clubs should be approached for information. Possibly the leading crags are Helsby, Stanage, Castle Naze, Brassington and Wharncliffe.

Guide books have now been written to most of them but are only accessible in Club Journals.

Lakeland

The Lake district of Cumberland, Westmorland and north Lancashire was the birthplace of British rock climbing and is still the principal centre if we judge by the number of people climbing there. The rock is of the very best kind for the purpose, igneous and much of it in the form of a dense and hard rhyolite.

The leading cliffs are:—

	most easily accessible from.
Great Gable	Wasdale or Borrowdale
Scafell	,, ,,
Pillar Rock	Wasdale or Ennerdale
Dow Crag	Coniston
Gimmer Crag	Langdale
Pavey Ark	,,
Deer Bield Crag	,,
Bowfell	,,
Harrison Stickle	,,
Raven Crag	,,
Middlefell Buttress	,,
Esk Buttress	Wasdale or Eskdale
Burtness Coombe	Buttermere

There are also a great number of smaller crags distributed over the whole area. Details of the available guidebooks are given in Chapter 11.

The best centres are Wasdale Head and Upper Langdale, but many prefer to stay in Borrowdale or Buttermere. Also for Dow Crag it makes life easier to stay in Coniston or camp by Goats Water. Owing to the configuration of the district it is not easy to change from one valley to another except by walking over the tops since fortunately there are few through roads.

North Wales

The many cliffs in North Wales are in general larger and often looser than the Lakes cliffs. The whole district is more mountainous and the valleys harsher in aspect. The hardest climbs in North Wales tend to be longer and less artificial than the hardest climbs in the Lakes. A climb is termed artificial if it is not distinct from other climbs or if it is possible to escape from it on to easier rock when once started.

The chief climbing grounds are:—

	most easily accessible from
Glyder Fach	Ogwen
Glyder Fawr	"
Idwal Slabs	"
The Gribin	"
Bochlwyd Buttress	"
Y Garn	"
Ysgolion Duon	"
Craig yr Ysfa	" or Gwern y gof
Tryfan	" "
Gallt yr Ogof	" "
Lliwedd	Pen y Pass
Crib Goch	"
Dinas Mot	" or Ynys Ettws
Clogwyn y Ddisgl	" "
Craig Cwm Beudy Mawr	" "
Dinas Cromlech	" "
Carreg Wastad	" "
Clogwyn y Grochan	" "
Gyrn Las	" "
Clogwyn du'r Arddu	" Llanberis or Rhyd-du
Mynydd Mawr	Rhyd-du or Nantlle
Nantlle y Garn	" " "
Cwm Silin	Nantlle
Cader Idris	Dolgelley

Centres are less well defined than in the Lakes and are less necessary as unfortunately many main roads run through the mountain area, and make it possible and easy to climb on any mountain in the area if a car or bicycle is available. The most popular centre is the Nant Ffrancon where there are many good farms to stay in, an excellent youth hostel at Idwal, and two climbing huts, Helyg and Glan Dena. For the Snowdon massif there are again farms and hostels all round from Capel Curig to Beddgelert and Llanberis, as well as a good youth hostel at the latter place. For Cader Idris there are hotels in Dolgelley and at Tal y Llyn on its eastern flank.

Scotland

To list all the mountains on which good climbing and walking is to be found in Scotland would swell the size of the book considerably, and it is necessary to restrict the list and only to mention the more popular places. The type of rock varies widely through the whole gamut from gabbro to limestone.

THE ARROCHAR GROUP

The Cobbler
Beinn Narnain
A'Chrois

These are most easily accessible from Arrochar. They give a large number of relatively short climbs and are hardly representative of the best Scottish climbing; however they have the merit of extreme accessibility from Glasgow and the Lowlands.

THE GLENCOE GROUP

Buchaille Etive Mor	Gearr Aonach
Bidean nan Bian	Beinn Fhada
Stob Coire nan Lochan	An-t-Sron
Stob Coire nan Beith	Aonach Eagach
Aonach Dubh	Sron na Creise

These are most easily accessible from Kingshouse or Clachaig.

BEN NEVIS (most easily accessible from Fort William or Glen Nevis).

CARN DEARG (most easily accessible from Fort William or Glen Nevis).

CREAG MHEAGAIDH (most easily accessible from Laggan).

LOCHNAGAR (most easily accessible from Balmoral).

CAIRNGORMS (most easily accessible from Aviemore or Braemore).

The rock climbing in this group is chiefly on Coire Brochain, Sgoran Dubh, Creag Coire an Lothain and Beinn a'Bhuird.

THE TORRIDON GROUP, Beinn Eighe, Liathach, Beinn Alligin, Beinn Dearg and Slioch (most easily accessible from Kinlochewe).

THE DUNDONNELL GROUP. An Teallach (most easily accessible from Dundonnell where there is a convenient and comfortable inn).

Beinn Dearg Mhor (most easily accessible from Strath na Shealleag).

SKYE.

Sgurr Alasdair	Sgurr Dearg
Sgurr Sgumain	Gars Bheinn
Am Bhasteir	Sgurr nan Gillean
Sgurr a Mhadaidh	Bruach na Frithe
Sgurr na L'Uamha	

These are accessible from Sligachan, or better from Glenbrittle, where there is now a new youth hostel.

ARRAN.

Cir Mhor	A'Chir
Ben Nuis	Beinn Tarsuinn
Caisteal Abhail	

These are most easily accessible from Brodick or Corrie.

Chapter 10

HOSTELS AND CLIMBING HUTS

MOST climbers in this country find it more pleasant as well as much less expensive to stay in climbing huts or youth hostels while climbing rather than in hotels or lodging houses. The chief advantage is the greater freedom of action and movement conferred on the climbing party by their use, as British hotels, pretty well without exception, demand that their guests should be in at definite times for meals and are unwilling to change their routine to meet the demands of climbers. This is especially annoying in good weather in summer when parties will want to leave early in the morning and return after sunset.

Most of the leading clubs therefore provide huts for the use of their members, and of members of kindred clubs, in climbing districts, and the gaps are filled by the very excellent hostels of the Youth Hostels Association which are open to all by joining the Association.

The following huts are available—the word hut being an understatement, most of them being very well equipped cottages.

North Wales

Helyg, nr. Capel Curig. (Property of the Climbers' Club but open to Cambridge University Mountaineering Club, Oxford University Mountaineering Club, Fell and Rock Climbing Club, Wayfarers' Club and Scottish Mountaineering Club).

Ynys Ettws, nr. Llanberis. (Now building.)

Pinnacle Club Hut, Cwm Dyli. (Property of the Pinnacle Club but open to Ladies' Alpine Club.)

Glan Dena. (Property of the Midland Association of Mountaineers.)

Tyn-y-weirglodd, Rhyddu. (Property of the Manchester University Mountaineering Club.)

Lake District

Brackenclose, Wasdale. (Property of Fell and Rock Climbing Club but open to Climbers' Club, Wayfarers' Club, Rucksack Club and Scottish Mountaineering Club.)

Raw Head, Langdale. (Property of Fell and Rock Climbing Club, but open to Climbers' Club.)

Robertson Lamb Hut, Langdale. (Property of Wayfarers' Club but open to Climbers' Club, Fell and Rock Climbing Club, Rucksack Club.)

Scotland

C.I.C. Memorial Hut, Ben Nevis. (Property of Scottish Mountaineering Club but open to the Junior Mountaineering Club of Scotland and by prior arrangement to members of other kindred clubs.)

Laggan Garbh, Glencoe. (Property of Scottish Mountaineering Club, but open to Junior Mountaineering Club of Scotland.)

Steill, Glen Nevis. (Property of Junior Mountaineering Club of Scotland.)

Cornwall

Bosigran, nr. St. Ives. (Property of the Climbers' Club but open to Cambridge University Mountaineering Club, Oxford University Mountaineering Club, Fell and Rock Climbing Club, Wayfarers' Club and Rucksack Club.)

As these huts do not have resident wardens, the comfort and civilisation of living in them depends to a very large extent on the co-operation of the people using them. There are no standard rules for their use because local conditions and their equipment vary considerably. The guiding rule is that each party should do more than it considers its fair share of the chores of housekeeping, and that the particular rules made by the hut warden, and usually posted up in the hut, are observed in the spirit as well as in the letter.

Chapter 11

CLIMBING GUIDE BOOKS AND LITERATURE

MOUNTAINEERING AND ROCK CLIMBING GUIDE BOOKS. In order to meet a great demand, various British Clubs have produced detailed guide books to rock climbs and mountaineering in these Islands.

A list is given below of the principal books of this kind which have been published.

SCOTTISH MOUNTAINEERING CLUB GUIDE BOOKS

1. General. Out of print.
2. Ben Nevis. Price 8/6d.
3. Island of Skye. Out of print.
4. Cairngorms. Out of print.
5. Western Highlands. Out of print.
6. Northern Highlands. Price 7/6d.
7. Central Highlands. Out of print.
8. The Islands (excluding Skye). Price 6/6d.
9. Guide to Cobbler Climbs. Price 1/3d.

The above guidebooks are obtainable from Messrs. Douglas and Foulis, 9 Castle Street, Edinburgh.

FELL AND ROCK CLIMBING CLUB GUIDE BOOKS TO THE LAKE DISTRICT

1. Pillar Rock and neighbourhood, by H. M. Kelly. Price 2/6d.
2. Scafell, by A. T. Hargreaves. Price 2/6d.
3. Gable, Buttermere and Borrowdale, by C. J. A. Cooper, E. Wood Johnson and L. Pollitt. Price 2/6d.
4. Langdale and Dow Craig. Price 3/6d.

These guide books are obtainable from the Cloister Press, Heaton Mersey, Manchester.

CLIMBERS' CLUB GUIDE BOOKS TO NORTH WALES.

1. Cwm Idwal, by J. M. Edwards. Price 5/6d.
2. Tryfan, by J. M. Edwards and C. W. F. Noyce. Price 5/6d.
3. Glyder Fach, by C. F. Kirkus. Price 5/6d.

4. Lliwedd, by C. W. F. Noyce and J. M. Edwards. Price 5/6.
5. Clogwyn du'r Arddu, by J. M. Edwards and J. E. Q. Barford. Price 2/9d.
6. Craig yr Ysfa, by A. D. M. Cox and H. E. Kretschmer. Price 2/9d.
7. Three Cliffs in Llanberis, by J. E. Q. Barford. Price 2/9d.

These guide books are also obtainable if in print from Cloister Press Ltd., Heaton Mersey, Manchester, or any bookseller.

These guide books vary widely in character according to the publishing club and to the style and opinions of the individual writers.

With the exception of the Cobbler guide book, the Scottish Mountaineering Club guides are much wider in their scope than the others, giving details of foot-paths and routes across the mountains as well as of rock and snow climbs.

The Fell and Rock and the Climbers' Club guides are more specialised and describe in great detail the rock climbs of the Lake District and North Wales, telling how to find and follow climbs, in some cases how to climb them and classifying their difficulty.

Because of the differences in the views of individual authors, grading of climbs has become a matter of considerable controversy and the method of grading differs greatly both between authors of guide books published by one club, and between different clubs, and in the system used. Therefore until you have become familiar with the style of a particular author, it is advisable to take the classifications of degree with a grain of salt. Because in district A or on cliff X it is quite within your powers to climb routes graded "very difficult" do not assume that in district B or on cliff Y you can do climbs described in the same way even if you yourself are on similar form and the weather is good. It is best to view every author of a guide book as human and fallible and trust one's own judgment.

To complicate the matter still further, there are five distinct methods of classification in use. These are as follows:—

The Skye System

The climbs described in the Skye guide book are graded 1, 2, 3, 4 and 4A in ascending order of difficulty. Comparisons with other districts are made very difficult indeed owing to the unique qualities of Skye rock.

Scottish Mainland System

In some of the Scottish guide books, where rock climbs have been described in considerable detail, a system of classification which is a modification of the original Lakeland system has been adopted. The grades used are easy, difficult, very difficult and severe.

In the more recent books published by the Scottish Mountaineering club, a further grade termed "Amiable severe" has been introduced between "very difficult" and "severe."

Lakeland System

This system is developed from one proposed and used by Owen Glynne Jones.

This system has formed the basis of most of the classifications of English rock climbs for the past 40 years. The grades now in common use are easy, moderate, difficult, very difficult, severe, very severe and are supplemented in the guide books by graded lists of climbs in ascending order of difficulty.

Numerical System

This system is the result of a recent attempt to rationalise the classification and so far has only been used in the war-time guide books issued by the Climbers' Club and in certain articles in the Climbers' Club Journal and the

Rucksack Club Journal. It has been developed in order to distinguish easily between the climbs in the higher grades.

The standards adopted are:—

I. Easy or moderate.
II. Difficult.
III. Very difficult.
IV. Severe.
V. Very severe (technically).
VI. Very severe.

The last grade has been introduced to cover the "great" routes which have other outstanding qualities apart from technical difficulty, such as extreme exposure, non-artificiality, and great length or objective dangers such as loose rock.

Some authors use this system and sub-divide the grades by using suffixes A & B. If it is IVA it would be a mild severe—IVB a hard severe and so on.

OTHER BOOKS. The book which every serious or carefree enthusiast reads is "Mountain Craft" by Geoffrey Winthrop Young, of which a new edition has recently been published by Methuen. This is the standard work on greater mountaineering and is accepted as such throughout the world.

Other books on technique are:—

The Technique of Alpine Mountaineering : translated by E. A. M. Wedderburn and published by the Association of British Members of the Swiss Alpine Club.
Mountaineering on foot and on ski : E. A. M. Wedderburn.
Mountaineering : The Badminton Library. Edited by C. T. Dent.
Mountaineering : The Lonsdale Library. Edited by Sidney Spencer.
Mountaineering : T. A. H. Peacocke.
The Handbook of American Mountaineering : Henderson.

There have also been many books giving accounts of climbs and descriptions of the mountain scene in these islands.

Amongst these are:—

Hillwritings of J. H. Doughty.
Always a Little Further, by Alastair Borthwick.
Lets go Climbing : C. F. Kirkus.

Climbing Days : Dorothy Pilley.
British Hills and Mountains : Bell and Bozman.

An even greater number of books have been written of climbing in the Alps, the Himalaya and other ranges of varying quality, and some dealing only with one expedition. The following may be mentioned:—

The Romance of Mountaineering : R. L. G. Irving.
The Mountain Way—An Anthology : R. L. G. Irving.
The Englishman in the Alps. An Anthology by Arnold Lunn.
The Making of a Mountaineer : G. I. Finch.
The Mountains of Youth by Arnold Lunn.
Days of Fresh Air : L. S. Amery.
Peaks and Pleasant Pastures : Claud Schuster.
High Conquest : J. R. Ullman.
The Alps : R. L. G. Irving.
Adventures of an Alpine Guide : Klucker.
Alpine Pilgrimage : Julius Kugy.
My Climbs in the Alps and the Caucasus : Mummery.
The Playground of Europe : Leslie Stephen.
Norway, the Northern Playground : W. Cecil Slingsby.
Scrambles in the Alps : Whymper.
The Alps in 1864 : A. W. Moore.
Wandering in the High Alps : Wills.
On High Hills : G. Winthrop Young.
An Alpine Journey : F. S. Smythe.
Climbs and Ski Runs : F. S. Smythe.
Brenva : T. Graham Brown.
Approach to the Hills : C. F. Meade.
Climbs on Mont Blanc : de Lépiney.
Upon that Mountain : Eric Shipton.
Kangchenjunga Adventure : F. S. Smythe.
Kamet Conquered : F. S. Smythe.
After Everest : Howard Somervell.
Everest 1933 : Routledge.
Nanda Devi : Eric Shipton.
Blank on the Map : Eric Shipton.
The Ascent of Nanda Devi : H. W. Tilman.
Snow on the Equator : H. W. Tilman.
Helvellyn to Himalaya : F. Spencer Chapman.

Technical Books and Articles.

Knots, Ties and Splices, by Commander J. Irving, gives all the information which the climber needs on knots with the exception of the prusik knot.

The following technical articles have appeared in Journals and are included here for completeness:—

FRCCJ	Vol.	10	Rope Management	... A. T. Hargreaves
MJ	Vol.	1	Modern Icecraft	... L. Maduschka
MJ	Vol.	4	The Prusik Knot	... M. Debelakova
RCJ	Vol.	8	Use the Rope ...	... A. S. Pigott
,,	,,		After the Accident	... Wilson Hey
SMCJ	Vol.	20	Climbing Down ...	... C. W. Parry
,,	,,		Roping Down ...	... E. A. M. Wedderburn
CCJ (NS)	Vol.	4	The Strength of Ropes	... A. L. Bird
CCJ (NS)	Vol.	6	On the requisite strength of a climbing rope	... B. L. Goodsell
CCJ (NS)	Vol.	7	Accidents in the Welsh Hills	... J. A. Martinez
AJ	Vol.	43	Report on Rope	
AJ	Vol.	44	Report on Rope	

FRCCJ Fell and Rock Climbing Club Journal.
MJ Mountaineering Journal.
RCJ Rucksack Club Journal.
SMCJ Scottish Mountaineering Club Journal.
CCJ Climbers' Club Journal.
AJ Alpine Journal.

Appendix I

GLOSSARY OF GAELIC, NORSE AND WELSH WORDS IN THE PLACE-NAMES OF GREAT BRITAIN

I. GAELIC.

In Gælic the stress accent falls on the first syllable, except in compound names, where the chief stress falls on the qualifying word. The aspirated digraphs 'bh' and 'mh' are represented by 'v' in English; 'fh' is silent; 'ch' is equivalent to the guttural sound heard in the German word *Nacht*.

In the respelt word the vowels have the following phonetic values; 'a' as in 'father,' 'ä' as in 'shake,' ' 'â as in 'all,' 'e' as in 'pen,' 'ē' as in 'feet,' 'ê' as in 'where,' 'i' as in 'tin,' 'ī' as in 'time,' 'o' as in 'cot,' 'ō' as in 'mote' 'oo' as in 'foot,' 'ow' as in 'cow,' 'u' as in 'tub,' and 'ū' as in 'tube.' Of the consonants 'g' is always hard as in 'gate.'

The definite article varies according to gender, number, case and the initial letter of the noun to which it is prefixed; its forms are am, an, an t-, a', na, na h-, nam, nan.

Aber, Abar, Obar, mouth or confluence of a river.
Abhainn, Amhuinn (*pron.* av′-uin), river. Usually **Avon.**
Acair, Acarsaid (*pron.* ach′-gur, ach′-gur-sad), anchor, anchorage; harbour.
Achadh (*pron.* ach′-a), field, park. Usually **Ach.**
Ailean (*pron.* al′-yen), a green place; plain.
Airidh (*pron.* ar′-ē), sheiling.
Aisir (*pron.* ash′-ir), a rocky defile or pass.
Allt (*pron.* âlt), brook, burn, stream. Conventional forms: **Ald, Alt, Auld, Ault.**
Aoineadh (*pron.* uen′-a), a steep promontory or brae.
Ard, Aird, a high point, promontory.
Ath (*pron.* ah), a ford; also a kiln.
Avon, conventional form of **Abhainn,** *q.v.*

Bad (*pron.* bât) a thicket, tuft.
Bagh (*pron.* bâh), a bay.
Baile (*pron.* bal′-y), town. Usually **Bal, Bali.**
Ban, white, fair. **Ban-Righ.** Queen.
Barp, conical heap of stones, a chambered cairn.
Barr, a point, top, extremity.
Bard, a poet; a dyke, enclosure, ward.
Beag (*pron.* bāk), little, small. Conventional form, **Beg.**
Bealach (*pron.* byall′ach), breach, pass, gap.
Bean (pron. ben), housewife, plural, **Ban.**
Beinn (*pron.* byān), a mountain. Conventional form: **Ben.**
Beith (*pron.* bā), a birch tree.
Beul (*pron.* biol), a mouth.
Binnean or **Binnein** (*pron.* bin′-en), a pinnacle, little mountain.
Blar, a plain, battlefield.
Bo, plural **Ba**, cow, cows.
Bodach (*pron.* bott′-ach), an old man, hobgoblin, spectre.
Bog (*pron.* bok), soft, miry, damp.
Both, Bothan (*pron.* bo, bo′-han), a hut, booth or brothy.
Bradan (*pron* (brat′-han), a salmon.
Braigh (*pron.* brai′-h), top, summit. Usually **Brae, Bread.**
Breac (*pron.* brechk), spotted, pie-bald, speckled, trout.
Broc (*pron.* broch), a badger.
Bruaich (*pron.* broo′-ach), a bank, brae, brim, steep place.
Buachaille (*pron.* buo′-ach-ilyu), a herdsman.
Buidhe (*pron.* boo′-i), yellow, golden coloured.
Bun, a root, bottom, mouth of a river.
Burn, a stream: *Anglo-Saxon*, Burne.
Cadha (*pron.* ka′-a), a pass, steep path.
Cailleach (*pron.* kyl′-ach), a nun, old woman.
Cala or **Caladh** (*pron.* ka′-la), a harbour.
Carn, a heap of stones, cairn.
Cam (*pron.* cam), crooked, bent, one-eyed.
Camas (*pron.* ka′-mas), bay, bend, channel.
Caol (*pron.* kaol), strait, firth, narrow. Other form **Kyle.** Alternative Gaelic form: **Gaolas.**
Carr, broken ground.
Ceann (*pron.* kyenn), head, headland. Usually **Ken, Kin.**
Ceapach, a tillage plot.
Ceo (*pron.* kyō), fog, mist.
Cill (*pron.* kil), a cell, church. Usually **Kil.**
Cioch (*pron.* kioch), a pap, woman's breast.
Clach (*pron.* klach), a stone. **Clachan,** stones, hamlet.
Cladach (*pron.* klad′-ach), shore, beach.
Cladh (*pron.* klugh), a churchyard, a burying ground.
Clais, a hollow.
Cleit (*pron.* klājt), a ridge, reef; rocky eminence.
Cluain, a field, pasture, green plain, meadow.
Cnap (*pron.* krap), a knob, hillock.
Cnoc (*pron.* knochk, krochk), a knoll. Usually **Knock.**

Coill or **Coille** (*pron.* kolyi), a wood, forest.
Coire (*pron.* kor′-e), a cauldron, kettle, circular hollow. Other form: **Corry.**
Creag (*pron.* krāg), a rock, cliff.
Crioch (*pron.* krēoch), boundary, frontier, landmark.
Cro, a sheep-fold, pen.
Crom, bent, sloping, crooked.
Cruach (*pron.* kroo′-ach), stack, heap, haunch.
Cul (*pron.* kool), the back, a nook.
Dail (*pron.* dal), a field. In Norse, a dale.
Damh (*pron.* day), a bullock, heifer.
Darach, oak, oak wood.
Dearg, red.
Doire, grove, hollow.
Druim, the back, ridge. Usually **Drem, Drom, Drum.**
Dubh (*pron.* doo), black, dark. Other form: **Dhu.**
Dun (*pron.* doon), a fort, castle, heap.
Eaglais(*pron.* āklash), a church, temple.
Each, Eich, a horse.
Ear, east.
Eas (*pron.* es), a waterfall. Other form: **Easach** (*pron.* es′-ach), a cascade.
Easg (*pron.* āsk), bog, fen, natural ditch.
Eilean (*pron.* ēl′-an), an island.
Fad, long, *e.g.*, **Beinn Fhada**, long mountain.
Faoghail, a ford, sea channel.
Feadan, narrow glen.
Fear (*pron.* fer), a man, husband, individual.
Fearn (*pron.* fern), an alder tree.
Feith (*pron.* fā), bog, sinewy stream, a vein.
Fiadh (*pron.* fee′-ugh), a deer.
Fuar (*pron.* foo′-ar), cold.
Fuaran (*pron.* fou-ar′-an), a perennial spring, well.
Gabhar or **Gobhar** (*pron.* go′-ur), a goat.
Garbh (*pron.* garv), rough. Other spelling: **Garve.**
Garadh (*pron.* ga′-ra), a fence, dike, garden.
Geal (*pron.* gel), white, clear, bright.
Geodha (*pron.* goe), a narrow creek, chasm, rift, cove.
Glas, grey, pale, wan; green. **Glais,** a stream.
Glac, a hollow, dell, defile.
Gleann (*pron.* glyan′), narrow valley, dale, dell. Usually **Glen.**
Gob, point, beak.
Gualann (*pron.* gwal′-in), shoulder of a mountain or hill.
I (*pron.* ē), an island.
Inbhir (*pron.* in′-ver), confluence, place at the meeting of river and sea. Other form: **Inver,** *c.f.*, **Aber.**
Innis (*pron.* in′-ish), island, meadow. Usually Inch.
Ken, Kin, *see* **Ceann.**
Kil, *see* **Cil.**
Knock, *see* **Cnoc.**

Kyle, *see* **Caol** and **Caolas.**
Lag (*pron.* lak), a hollow in a hill. Usually **Logan, Logie.**
Lairig, the sloping face of a hill, a pass.
Leaba (*pron.* lya′-ba) a bed, couch, lair.
Leathad (*pron.* le′-ud), a slope, declivity.
Leathan (*pron.* lyā′-un), broad.
Leitir, a slope.
Liath (*pron.* lēa), grey.
Linne (*pron.* lyēn′-a), a pool, sound, channel.
Lios (*pron.* lēs), a garden.
Loch, a lake, arm of the sea. **Lochan,** small loch.
Lon, a marsh, morass.
Lub (*pron.* loob), a bend, fold, curvature.
Machair (*pron.* mach′-ar), a plain or extensive beach.
Magh, a field, plain.
Mam, a round or gently rising hill.
Maol (*pron.* mull), headland, bald top, cape.
Meadhon (*pron.* me′-un), middle, central.
Meall (*pron.* myal), knob, lump, rounded hill.
Min (*pron.* mēn), smooth, soft, delicate.
Monadh (*pron.* mon′-a), moor, heath, hill, mountain.
Mod, a court of justice, meeting, small knoll.
Moine or **Mointeach** (*pron.* mò′-en-tyach), moss-land, mossy.
Mor, great, large, tall. English form: **More.**
Muc (*pron.* moocht), a sow, pig. Usually **Muck, Muick.**
Muileann (*pron.* mool′-an), mill.
Muir (*pron.* mur), the sea.
Murach (*pron.* moor′-ach), a down or sandhill on the sea shore.
Muran, sea bent.
Nathair, Nathraichean, serpent.
Ob, a bay, creek, haven. Other form: **Tob.**
Odhar (*pron.* ō′-ur), dapple, drab, dun-coloured, sallow.
Oitir (*pron.* oj′-tyer), sandbank, shoal, shallow, bar, reef.
Or, gold.
Ord, a round steep, or conical hill.
Os (*pron.* ōs), outlet of a lake or river.
Pit or **Pet,** farm, hollow.
Poll (*pron.* poul), a pool, pond, pit.
Rathad (*pron.* ra′-ud), a road, way.
Reidh (*pron.* rā), plain, level, smooth.
Riabhach (*pron.* rē′-ach), drab, greyish, brindled, grizzled. Other form: **Riach.**
Righ (*pron.* rē), a king. Other form: **Ree.**
Roinn, a point, headland, peninsula.
Ros, a point, promontory. Other form: **Ross.**
Ruadh (*pron.* roo′-a), red, reddish.
Rudha (*pron.* roo′-a), promontory. Usually **Ru, Rhu, Row.**
Ruigh, a run for cattle, sheiling, land sloping.
Sagart (*pron.* sa′-kart), a priest.
Sail, a heel.

Sean (*pron.* shen), old, aged, ancient.
Seileach (*pron.* shāl′-ach), a willow.
Sgeir (*pron.* skeir), a reef, sea-surrounded rock.
Sgorr or **Sgurr** (*pron.* skor, skoor), a peak, conical sharp rock. Sometimes **Scaur.**
Sith (*pron.* shē), a fairy. **Sithean** (*pron.* shee′-an), a fairy hillock or knoll.
Slochd, a deep hollow.
Sneachd (*pron.* snyachg), snow.
Srath (*pron.* stra), a valley, plain beside a river, strath.
Sron, nose, peak, promontory. Other form: **Strone.**
Sruth (*pron.* stru), a stream, current. Usually **Struan.**
Stac (*pron.* stak), a steep rock, conical hill.
Stob (*pron.* stop), a point.
Stuc (*pron.* stook), a pinnacle, peak, conical steep rock
Suidhe (*pron.* sooi′-ye), sitting, resting place.
Tairbeart (*pron.* tar′-pyart), an isthmus. Other forms: **Tarbet, Tarbert.**
Taigh or **Tigh** (*pron.* ty), a house. Usually **Tay, Ty.**
Tir (*pron.* tyēr), country, region, land. Other form: **Tyr.**
Tobar, a well, spring, fountain. Usually **Teber.**
Tom (*pron.* tōm), a hillock, mound.
Torc (*pron.* tork), a boar.
Torr, a mound, heap, hill.
Traigh (*pron.* try), sea-shore, beach, strand, sands.
Tulach (*pron.* too′-ach), knoll, hillock, eminence. Anglicized forms: **Tilly, Tully, Tulloch.**
Uachdar (*pron.* ooach′-ur), upper-land. Usually **Auchter, Ochter.**
Uaine (*pron.* ooin′-e), green.
Uamh (*pron.* oo′-av), a cave, a grave.
Uchd (*pron.* oochg), ascent, face of a hill.
Uig (*pron.* ooēg), a nook, bay.
Uisge, water, rain.

II. NORSE.

A, Ay, A, island, *e.g.*, Soa, sheep isle, Pabby priest's isle.
Ager, Acker, arable or cultivated land.
Bard, extremity, point, headland.
Beck, a brook.
Bogha or **Bodha,** a sunk rock.
Bost, farmhouse, dwelling.
Brochs, circular dry stone supposed Pictish buildings.
By, village, town.
Carse, alluvial fertile land alongside a river.
Ey, an island. *See* **Ay.**
Fair, Far (*Norwegian,* **Faar**), sheep.
Fell, Field (*Norwegian,* **Fjeld**), mountain.
Firth, Frith (*Lat.* **Fretum**), strait, estuary of a river.
Gill, a ravine.

Gio, a chasm, rift.
Grind, a gate.
Holm, an island in river or sea near the shore.
Hope, an inner bay. **Gob,** *e.g.*, Oban.
How (Haugr), a burial mound.
Law, a conical hill.
Lax, a salmon.
Mol, shingly beach. **Mol.**
Nab (*Norwegian*, **Knab**), a rock projection.
Ness, a point, headland.
Noup, a lofty headland.
Papa, spiritual father, a prefix to several of the Orkney and Shetland Islands.
Skerries, isolated rocks or islets.
Stack, a columnar rock.
Stor, Stour, big, large, great.
Thing, Ting, a provincial parliament.
Toft, enclosed home-field.
Vik, Wik, a creek.
Voe, a little bay, inlet.
Whal (*Norwegian*, **Hval**), a whale.

III. WELSH.

THE pronunciation of Welsh is greatly simplified by an understanding of the following points:

(*a*) The language is almost completely phonetic.

(*b*) All consonants are pronounced and always in the same way.

(*c*) The seven vowels, a, e, i, o, u, w, y, each have their own sounds, which they retain with a slight slurring effect when joined together as diphthongs.

a	long as in English " half " short as in English " hat "
e	long as in English " wait " (North-Country) short as in English " wet "
i	long as in English " seat " short as in English " sit "
o	long as in English " coat " short as in English " cot "
u	almost the same as long i
w	long as in English " tomb " short as in English " foot "
*y	" boscure " as English u or o in " undone " long as the Welsh u short as the short Welsh i

*Of these three sounds the first is the most common. The second and third are only met in words of one syllable and in the last syllable of longer words. Exceptions are the definite article " y " or " yr," the preposition " yn " meaning " in " and the possessive adjectives " fy " and " dy " meaning " my " and " thy," all of which have the so-called obscure sound as " uh," " err " " un," " vuh " and " duh."

(*d*) of the consonants, the following alone need comment.

c.	always hard as in " cat "
ch.	as in Gaelic or German " ach " or " och;" never as in church or ache.
dd.	as English " th " in " this "
f.	always as English " of "
ff.	always as English " off "
g.	always hard as in " gun "
ll.	no parallel in English
r.	always trilled slightly, e.g., a Welshman would emphasise the difference in pronunciation between English " father " and " farther "
s.	always strong as in " sister," never as in " busy "
th.	as English " th " in " think "

(*e*) Certain initial consonants of words undergo mutation according to fixed laws. The types likely to be met in place names are:—

c softens	to g	e.g.,	carreg to garreg
p ,,	to b	,,	pont to bont
t ,,	to d	,,	tre to dre
g disappears		,,	gallt to allt
b softens	to f	,,	bach to fach
d ,,	to dd	,,	dysgl to ddysgl
ll ,,	to l	,,	llyn to lyn
m ,,	to f	,,	moel to foel
rh ,,	to r	,,	rhyd to ryd

(*f*) The accent falls almost variably on the penultimate syllable as in English " moment'-ous."

Aber, estuary, river mouth.
Aderyn, bird.
Ael, brow, edge.
Afanc, beaver, a fabulous monster.
Afon, river.
Aran, garden.
Arddu, very black.
Bach, little, small.
Ban, peak.
Bedd, grave.
Bere, kite.
Bettws, probably = A.S. beadhouse—chapel.
Beudy, cowhouse.

Blaen, point, top, pl. Blaenau—upper reaches.
Boch, cheek.
Bod, dwelling, abode.
Braich, arm.
Bras, rich, fertile.
Brith (f) **Braeth,** pied, speckled.
Bron, breast.
Bryn, hill.
Brwynog, rushy, marshy, sad.
Bual, buffalo.
Bustach, bullock
Buwch, cow.
Bwlch, col, neck between two peaks.
Cadair, chair.
Cae, field.
Caer, camp, fort.
Cafn, trough.
Capel, chapel.
Carn
Carnedd } heap of stones, cairn, hill
Carreg (pl.) Cerrig, stone, rock.
Caseg, mare.
Castell, castle.
Ceffyl, horse.
Cefn, ridge, back.
Cidwm, wolf.
Clogwyn, cliff, precipice.
Clyd, warm, sheltered.
Cneifion (pl), flocks.
Coch, red.
Coed (pl), wood, trees.
Cors, bog, swamp.
Crach, dwarf.
Craig, crag, rock.
Crib, comb, ridge.
Cribin, rake.
Crochan, cauldron, pot.
Croes, cross.
Cromlech, probably from cryman, (sickle) and llech, q.v.
Cwm, hollow, valley head.
Cwn (pl. of **ci**), dogs.
Cwrwgl, coracle.
Cyfrwy, saddle (of a horse).
Cyngor, counsel or council.
(pl. cynghorion—counsels).
(pl. cynghorau—councils).
Dau, two.
Dinas, city, fortress.
Dol, meadow.

Drum or **Trum,** ridge, summit.
Drws, door.
Du, black.
Dwfr, dwr, water.
Dyffryn, valley.
Dysgl, dish.
Eglwys, church.
Eigion, bottom, depth.
Einio, to plait, weave.
Erw, acre.
Esgair, leg, ridge.
Ffordd, road.
Ffynnon, spring.
Gafr (pl. **Geifr**), goat.
Gallt, hill (N. Wales, wood (S. Wales).
Garth, garden, enclosure.
Gefail, smithy.
Glan, bank, shore.
Glas, blue.
Glyn, vale, glen.
Goleu, light.
Grug, heather.
Gwastad, level, smooth.
Gwaun, meadow.
Gwern, swamp, meadow, alder-grove.
Gweryd, moss, mould.
Gwrach, hag, witch.
Gwrhyd or **Gwyrd,** valour.
Gwyddfa, tomb.
Gwyn (f. **gwen**), white.
Gwynt, wind.
Hafod, summer dwelling.
Haul, sun.
Hebog, hawk.
Helyg (pl), willows.
Hen, old.
Hir, long.
Isaf, lowest.
Lon, lane.
Llan, church.
Llech, flat stone.
Llithrig, slippery.
Lloer, moon.
Llug, bright.
Llwyd, grey.
Llwyn, bush, grove.
Llyn, lake.
Llys, court, palace.
Maen, stone.
Maes, field.

Man, place.
March, stallion.
Marchog, knight, horseman.
Mawr, big, large.
Melin, mill.
Melyn (f.-**en**), yellow.
Miliast (f), greyhound
Mochyn (pl. **moch**), pig.
Moel, bare hill, hill.
Mor, sea.
Morfa, moor, marsh.
Mur, wall.
Mynydd, mountain.
Nant, brook, glen, gorge.
Newydd, new.
Oer, cold.
Ogof, cave.
Pair, cauldron.
Pant, valley, hollow.
Parc, park, enclosure.
Pen, head, top.
Pentref, village.
Perfedd, middle.
Person, parson, person.
Poeth, hot.
Pont, bridge
Porth, gate, port.
Pwll, pool.
Rhaiadr, waterfall.
Rhiw, hill, slope.
Rhos, moor, heath.
Rhyd, ford.
Saeth, arrow.
Sarn, causeway.
Tal, end.
Tomen, heap, mound.
Tref, town.
Tri, three.
Troed, foot.
Twll, hole.
Ty, house.
Uchaf, highest.
Un, one.
-wy, water.
Y, yr, the.
Yn, in.
Ynys, island.
Ysfa, longing, itching.
Yspytty, hospice.
Ystrad, dale.

Appendix II

A LIST OF BRITISH CLIMBING CLUBS

CLUB	SECRETARY
Alpine Club	Bryan Donkin, Alliance House, Caxton Street, London, S.W.1.
Alpine Ski Club	Wing Cdr. K. C. Smith, Mill House, Gt. Missenden, Bucks.
Association of British Members of the Swiss Alpine Club	M. N. Clarke, 125, Queen's Gate, London, S.W.7.
Birmingham University M.C. ...	D. A. Hanson, Guild of Undergraduate's Union, The University, Birmingham, 15.
Cairngorm Club	William Garden, 18, Golden Square, Aberdeen.
Cambridge University M.C. ...	G. H. Wiltshire, Christs College, Cambridge.
Climbers' Club	F. H. Keenlyside, c/o The Ministry of Transport, Berkeley Square House, London, W.1.
Corrie Club	John Ferguson, 2, Hawkhill Place, Perth Road, Dundee.
Creagh Dhu M.C.	Chas. MacPherson, 31, Corkerhill Road, Glasgow, S.W.2.
Derbyshire Pennine Club	H. E. Chatburn, Hall Croft, Hope, via Sheffield.
*Dundee Rambling Club	A. J. S. Stewart, 1, Marchfield Terrace, Dundee.
Edinburgh University M.C. ...	J. G. Parish, 12, Columba Road, Edinburgh, 4.
Etchachan Club	William Irvine, 33, Westholme Avenue, Aberdeen.

CLUB	SECRETARY
*Fell and Rock Climbing Club ...	J. C. Appleyard, Greystones, Torver, Coniston, Lancs.
Glasgow University M.C.	Drummond Ellis, 47, Battlefield Avenue, Glasgow, S.2.
*Grampian Club	Graham S. Ritchie, 3, Nelson Terrace, Dundee.
Gritstone Club	A. F. Falkingham, 6, Park View Terrace, Bradford.
*Imperial College M.C.	Miss M. Thornley, Imperial College Union, Prince Consort Road, London, S.W.7.
Junior Mountaineering Club of Scotland	Wm. Bennett, 28, Churchill Drive, Glasgow, W.1.
Karabiner Club	E. Flitcroft, 8, Newhall Road, Jericho, Bury.
†Ladies' Alpine Club	Mrs. George Starkey, 30, Fairholme Road, Ilford, Essex.
†Ladies' Scottish Climbing Club ...	Miss A. Smith, Addistoun, Ratho, Newbridge, Midlothian
Lancashire Climbing and Caving Club	L. Barlow, 11, Wyresdale Road, Bolton, Lancs.
Leeds University M.C.	Bernard Black, Medical School, Thoresby Place, Leeds, 1.
Liverpool University M.C. ...	Arnold Carsten, 40, Druidsville Road, Liverpool, 18.
Lomond Mountaineering Club ...	Malcolm Finlayson, 72, Waterloo Street, Glasgow, C.2.
Manchester University M.C. ...	H. S. Heaps, University Union, Oxford Road, Manchester, 15.
*Midland Association of Mountaineers	D. J. Munns, 13, Sandford Road, Moseley, Birmingham, 13.

Club	Secretary
Moray Mountaineering Club, ...	John Geddes, Forteath Avenue, Baile Ur, Elgin.
*Mountaineering Section of the Camping Club	J. H. Young, 5, Oatfield Road, The Knoll, Orpington, Kent.
Oxford University M.C.	Christopher Hancock, Worcester College, Oxford.
Peak Climbing Club, ...	H. C. Bryson, Farndish, Wellingborough, Northants.
†Pinnacle Club	Miss A. Wilson, 3, Richmond Hill, Bath, Somerset.
Royal Artillery Alpine Club ...	Major J. Waller, D.S.O., M.C., H.Q. 2 A.A. Group, East Camp, R.A.F. Station, Uxbridge.
Rucksack Club	J. E. Byrom, Highfield, Douglas Road, Hazel Grove, Cheshire.
Scottish Ski Club	W. R. Higginbotham, 45, Renfield Street, Glasgow, C. 2.
Scottish Mountaineering Club ...	J. Logan Aikman, 121, St. Vincent Street, Glasgow, C.2.
Tricouni Club	R. Haigh, 1676, Coventry Road, South Yardley, Birmingham, 26.
Troglodytes	J. Beacom, Jnr., 15, North Croft, Paisley, Renfrewshire.
Wayfarers' Club	R. Shaw, Glencoe, Heswall, Cheshire.
Yorkshire Ramblers' Club ...	D. Burrow, Lyngarth, King Lane, Alwoodley, Leeds.

OTHER CLUBS. In addition, there are a number of smaller purely local clubs, too numerous to list here: and every university has its own mountaineering club, membership of which is confined to the undergraduates of the university.

All the clubs in the list above marked with an asterisk are open to men and women, those marked with a dagger to women only, the remainder to men only.

Appendix III

ASSISTANCE AND EVACUATION

The Mountaineering Clubs have installed special stretchers for mountain use, medical supplies, and equipment at the following places:—

SCOTLAND

Crianlarich Area (including Ben More, Ben Lui, Ben Cruachan).

Thomas Stretcher and complete equipment at :—
POLICE STATION, CRIANLARICH. Tel. 222.

Place at which Ambulance should wait :—
Nearest point on road or at nearest bridge over river.

AMBULANCE : J. & D. Macgregor, Killin. Tel. : Killin 6,
or from Oban (see Glencoe area).

POLICE : CRIANLARICH. Tel. : Crianlarich 222.
DALMALLY. Tel. : Dalmally 15.

HOSPITALS : Stirling Royal Infirmary. Tel. : Stirling 16.
or Oban Cottage Hospital. Tel. : Oban 2544.
Edinburgh Royal Infirmary. Tel. : 26031.
Glasgow Royal Infirmary. Tel. : BEL 3535.

Glencoe Area

Thomas stretcher and complete equipment at :—
CLACHAIG HOTEL, GLENCOE. Tel. : Ballachulish 252.

Place at which Ambulance should wait :—

Buchaille Etive district — Coupal Bridge or Lagangarbh.
South Glencoe hills — Footbridge below Loch Triochatan.
North Glencoe hills ... Convenient point on Glencoe road.

AMBULANCE : St. John Ambulance Association, Oban.
or County Council Ambulance—
apply to Medical Officer of Health, County Buildings, Oban. Tel. : 2489 or 2511.
or Marshall & Pearson's Garage, Fort William. Tel. : 15.

Glencoe Area—*continued.*

POLICE : Ballachulish. Tel. : Ballachulish 222.

HOSPITAL : Belford Hospital. Tel. : Fort William 49.
or Oban Cottage Hospital. Tel. : Oban 2544.
(Auxiliary Hospital at Glencoe House is probably only temporary.)
Edinburgh Royal Infirmary. Tel. : 26031.
Glasgow Royal Infirmary. Tel. : BEL 3535.

Skye—Cuillin Hills

Thomas stretcher and complete equipment at :—

(1) GLENBRITTLE HOUSE. Tel. : Glenbrittle 2.

(2) SLIGACHAN HOTEL. Tel. Sligachan 1.

Place at which Ambulance should wait :—

Central and South Area — Glenbrittle House.
North Area — Sligachan.

AMBULANCE : Skye Transport. Tel. : Portree 25.

POLICE : Portree. Tel. : Portree 4.

HOSPITALS : Mackinnon Memorial Hospital. Tel. : Broadford 206.
Gesto Hospital. Tel. : Edinbane 2.
Belford Hospital, Fort William. Tel. : Fort William 49.
Northern Infirmary, Inverness. Tel. : Inverness 770.
Raigmore Hospital, Inverness. Tel. : Inverness 1600.

Ben Nevis

Thomas stretcher and complete equipment at :—

(1) MARSHALL AND PEARSON, West Highland Garage, Fort William. Tel. : Fort William 15.

(2) CHARLES INGLIS CLARKE HUT, Allt-a'-Mhuilinn.

ADDITIONAL EQUIPMENT : Stretcher at Belford Hospital.

Ask Mr. D. G. Duff, F.R.C.S., Belford Hospital (Fort William 49) to organize rescue.

Place at which Ambulance should wait :—

Achintee or Ben Nevis Distillery.

AMBULANCE : Mr. Grant, Marshall & Pearson's West Highland Garage. Tel. : Fort William 15.

POLICE : Tel. : Fort William 261.

HOSPITAL : Belford Hospital. Tel. : Fort William 49.

Cairngorms : Lochnagar

Stretchers and complete equipment at :—

1) COYLUMBRIDGE, AVIEMORE. With Mr. Grant, Merchant. Tel. : Aviemore 220.

2) LUI BEG, BRAEMAR. (Key at Derry Lodge, Braemar.) Mr. Beattie.

(3) POLICE STATION, BRAEMAR. Tel. 222.

(4) SPITTAL OF MUICK, GLEN MUICK. With Mr. J. Robertson.

Place at which Ambulance should wait :—

North Cairngorms — Coylumbridge, Aviemore.
North-east Cairngorms — Inchrory, Glen Avon.
South Cairngorms — Derry Lodge, Braemar.
Lochnagar — Gelder Shiel.
or other convenient point.

AMBULANCE : Ballater. (To be called through Police) Tel. : Ballater 26 *or* Duke of Gordon Hotel, Kingussie. (Temporary) Tel. : Kingussie 102.

POLICE : North Cairngorms, Aviemore. Tel. : Aviemore 222.
North-east Cairngorms, Tomintoul. Tel. : Tomintoul 222.
South Cairngorms, Braemar. Tel. : 222.
Lochnagar, Ballater. Tel. : Ballater 20.

LAKE DISTRICT

FIRST AID POSTS;—

1. WASTWATER HOTEL, WASDALE HEAD. No telephone.
   SUPERVISOR : Mr. J. R. Whiting.
   DOCTOR : Dr. J. M. Norman, Haverigg, Gosforth. Tel. : 21.
   AMBULANCE : Cumberland Motor Service. Tel. : Whitehaven 381-2.
   POLICE : Police Station, Gosforth. Tel. : 33.
   HOSPITALS : Whitehaven and West Cumberland Infirmary Tel. : Whitehaven 75.
   Cumberland Infirmary, Carlisle. Tel. : 590.
2. WASDALE HEAD HALL FARM. No telephone.
   SUPERVISOR : Mr. Martin.
   Services as for No. 1.
3. SCAWFELL HOTEL, ROSTHWAITE, BORROWDALE. Tel. : Borrowdale 8.
   SUPERVISOR : Capt. S. H. Badrock.
   DOCTOR : Dr. Cameron, Riverholm, Keswick. Tels. : 407 and 532.

LAKE DISTRICT.—*continued*

AMBULANCE : St. John Ambulance, Keswick. Tel. 21
Keswick Motor Co. Tel. : 60.

POLICE : Keswick Police Station. Tel. : 4.

HOSPITALS : Keswick Cottage Hospital' Tel. : 12.
Cumberland Infirmary, Carlisle. Tel. : 590.
Manchester Royal Infirmary. Tel.: Ardwick 1721.
Leeds General Infirmary. Tel. : Leeds 20455.
Liverpool Royal Infirmary. Tel. : Royal 1900.

ADDITIONAL EQUIPMENT : St. John Ambulance equipment at Mountain View, Seatoller. Tel. : Borrowdale 30.
Ordinary stretcher at Honister Quarries.
A.A. Box, Honister Top. Tel. Borrowdale 40. (Key at Youth Hostel nearby.)

Ordinary stretcher and First Aid case at St. John's box, Sty Head Pass.

4. YOUTH HOSTEL, GILLERTHWAITE FARM, ENNERDALE.

NEAREST TELEPHONE : Anglers' Inn, Ennerdale. Tel. : Lamplugh 202.

SUPERVISOR : Mr. Pernette.

POLICE : Ennerdale Bridge. Tel. : Lamplugh 222.

DOCTOR, AMBULANCE and HOSPITALS as for No. 1.

ADDITIONAL EQUIPMENT :
Ordinary stretcher at Youth Hostel Hut, Black Sail.

5. DUNGEON GHYLL OLD HOTEL, GREAT LANGDALE.
Tel. :. Grasmere 72.

SUPERVISOR : Mr. C. G. Bulman.

DOCTORS : Dr. J. H. Patterson, Meadfoot, Windermere. Tel. : 78.
Dr. A. F. Quarmby, Gale Cottage, Ambleside. Tel. : 26.

AMBULANCE : Police Station, Ambleside. Tel. : 18.

POLICE : Police Station, Langdale. Tel. : Grasmere 39. (½ mile east of Elterwater on Ambleside Road.)

HOSPITALS : Kendal Hospital. Tel. : 71.
Manchester Royal Infirmary. Tel. : Ardwick1721.
Leeds General Infirmary. Tel. : Leeds 20455.
Liverpool Royal Infirmary. Tel. : Royal 1900.

6. THE INSTITUTE, CONISTON.

SUPERVISOR : Mr. J. C. Appleyard, Greystones, Torver, Coniston. Tel. : 31.

Two rucksacks also kept at Hut by Dow Crags.

LAKE DISTRICT—*continued.*

DOCTOR : Dr. W. A. Bowdler, Oak How, Coniston. Tel. : 52.

AMBULANCE : Ulverston Cottage Hospital. Tel. : 61.

POLICE : Tel. : Coniston 51.

HOSPITALS : Ulverston Cottage Hospital. Tel. : 61.
North Lonsdale Hospital, Barrow-in-Furness. Tel. : 896.
Manchester Royal Infirmary. Tel.: Ardwick 1721.
Leeds General Infirmary. Tel. : Leeds 20455.
Liverpool Royal Infirmary. Tel. : Royal 1900.

7. GATESGARTH FARM, BUTTERMERE.

SUPERVISOR : Mr. Richardson.

TELEPHONES : Buttermere Hotel. Tel. : Buttermere 4.
A.A. Box, Honister Top. Tel. : Borrowdale 40.
(Key at Youth Hostel nearby.)
Services as for Borrowdale (No. 3).

The areas served by the First Aid Posts are usually self-evident. It is, however, recommended :

WASDALE HEAD AREA. Send to Wastwater Hotel (Post 1) unless it is known that BRACKENCLOSE (F. & R.C.C. Hut) is occupied and can supply helpers.

Borrowdale is eventually a better line of evacuation, and, though it may mean a longer carry, should always be chosen (if it is possible to use it) because of better telephone facilities and roads leading to a wider choice of hospital.

PILLAR ROCK. Send to Gillerthwaite (Post 4) and evacuate via Ennerdale.

If more help wanted telephone Scawfell Hotel (Post 3) at Borrowdale 38, or St. John's Ambulance at Keswick 21. For help from Wasdale telephone police at Gosforth 33 and ask for message to be sent to Wasdale Head.

NORTH WALES

FIRST AID POSTS:—

1. YOUTH HOSTEL, IDWAL COTTAGE (next to Ogwen Cottage)

SUPERVISOR : Mr. R. S. Duncombe.

TELEPHONE : At Public Telephone Box outside Hostel.
L.O.G. Ogwen 1. Ingoing calls can be made.

DOCTOR : Dr. I. Mostyn Williams, Bethesda. Tel. : 212.

AMBULANCE : Mr. Hughes. Tel. : Bangor 194.

NORTH WALES—*continued.*

POLICE : Tel. : Bethesda 220.

HOSPITALS : Caernarvon and Anglesey Infirmary, Bangor. Tel. : 490-491.
Liverpool Royal Infirmary. Tel. : Royal 1900.
Manchester Royal Infirmary. Tel.: Ardwick 1721.

2. CLIMBERS' CLUB HUT, HELYG, which is 1½ miles in the direction of Capel Curig from the point where the North Ridge of Tryfan comes down to the Holyhead Road. It is about 70 yards below the road on the right hand side and power lines lead to it across the road.

SUPERVISOR : None. If locked, key at Gwern-y-Gof Isaf Farm. No telephone.

Services as for No. 1.

3. PEN-Y-GWRYD HOTEL. Tel. : Llanberis 211.

SUPERVISOR : Mr. O. E. Riddett.

DOCTOR : Dr. I. Wynn Jones, Bodafon and Plas Coch, Llanberis. Tel. : 208.

AMBULANCE : Tel. : Llanberis 202.

POLICE : Tel. : Llanberis 222.

HOSPITALS : Caernarvon and Anglesey Infirmary, Bangor. Tel. : 490-491.
Liverpool Royal Infirmary. Tel. : Royal 1900.
Manchester Royal Infirmary. Tel.: Ardwick 1721.

If additional helpers are wanted, climbers may be staying at :—

RUCKSACK CLUB HUT. (Tin Hut by Chapel on Ogwen Road at Nant-y-Benglog.)
BRYN TYRCH HOTEL (Mr. Smith). Tel. : Capel 223.
SIABOD VILLA (Mrs. Roberts). Tel. : Capel 229.
TYN-Y-COED HOTEL. Tel. : Capel 231.
ROYAL HOTEL. Tel. : Capel 230.
PEN-Y-PASS HOTEL.
LLUGWY COTTAGE, Capel.
M.A.M. HUT, Glan Dena, Ogwen.

EAST FACE OF TRYFAN :

If Helyg (Post 2) is likely to be occupied send there.

Otherwise send to Idwal Cottage (Post 1).

CRAIG YR YSFA :

Send to Hafod-y-Rhiw on the East side of the lake in Cwm Eigiau. A private line connects Mr. Duffin there with the North Wales Electric Power Station, Dolgarrog (Tel. 207) and messages will be passed on. Ask for message to be sent to Mr. Riddett at Pen-y-Gwryd Hotel

NORTH WALES—*continued.*

(Tel. : Llanberis 211) for equipment and stretcher to be sent by car to Hafod-y-Rhiw by the narrow but usually practicable road from Tal-y-Bont. Alternatively transmit the same request to Mr. R. S. Duncombe at Idwal Cottage (Tel.: L.O.G. Ogwen 1). If extra helpers are wanted they might well be sought in Ogwen Valley. Detailed instructions for obtaining assistance are available at Hafod-y-Rhiw.

DOCTOR : Dr. Meurig Williams, Station Road, Llanrwst. Tel. : 36.

AMBULANCE : N. J. Stanley, Llanrwst. Tel. : 118. To wait at Hafod-y-Rhiw.

POLICE : Tel. : Dolgarrog 222.

HOSPITAL : Llandudno & District Cottage Hospital, Trinity Avenue, Llandudno. Tel. : 7471.

CLOGWYN DU'R ARDDU :

Send to the Victoria Hotel, Llanberis (Tel. 9) on main road almost opposite the Mountain Railway station and telephone to Mr. Riddett at Pen y Gwryd Hotel (Tel. : Llanberis 211) for equipment and helpers to be sent by car, which can usually reach Hafotty-Newydd Farm. To get there from Llanberis fork right from the Snowdon path, after third gate, at a point where a signpost points the way to Snowdon. From Hafotty Newydd to Clogwyn du'r Arddu is an easy hour. Alternatively telephone to Mr. R. S. Duncombe at Idwal Cottage (Tel.: L.O.G. Ogwen 1). Seek the co-operation of Police at Llanberis 222.

Services as for Pen y Gwryd Hotel (Post 3).

The Ambulance might wait at Hafotty Newydd.

4. GLASFRYN, Rhyd-ddu.

SUPERVISOR : Mr. F. H. Thompson. Tel. : Beddgelert 220.

Helpers may be found at M.U.M.C. Hut, Tyn-y-Weirglodd, Bettws Garmon.

MID-WALES

FIRST AID POST:—

CADER IDRIS AREA. Telephone to :

The Outward Bound Sea School, Brynmeddyg, Aberdovey. Tel. 22.

SUPERVISOR : Mr. J. M. Hogan, who will organize the rescue. This is a privately owned First Aid Post at which a Duff Mountain stretcher and complete equipment is kept. The owners have kindly agreed to respond to calls for assistance and will turn out with trained personnel in a car, and with the local ambulance.

MID-WALES—*continued.*

DOCTOR : Dr. H. R. Wright. Tel. : Aberdovey 73.

AMBULANCE : Commandant, Red Cross Detachment.
Tel. : Aberdovey 20.

POLICE : Tel. : Aberdovey 47.

HOSPITAL : Dolgelley & Barmouth Hospital. Tel.: Dolgelley 79.

ADDITIONAL ASSISTANCE : Dr. R. W. Edwards, Tyn-y-coed. Tel.: Dolgelley 16.
Dr. H. D. Owen, Caerffynnon. Tel.: Dolgelley 32.

AMBULANCE AND POLICE : Tel. : Dolgelley 203–4.

Places at which the Ambulance should wait :—

For accidents on the North side of Cader Idris :—

At the telephone box, marked Duffrydan on 1-in. map, about ½ mile west of Gwernan Lake and on the Cader Idris road from Dolgelley.

For accidents on the South side of Cader Idris :—
At telephone box at the west end of Tal-y-Llyn lake.

DERBYSHIRE

FIRST AID POST:—

HOPE, near Castleton.

Neil Robertson stretcher and two rucksacks of equipment in the custody of Dr. J. W. W. Baillie, Hope. Tel. : Hope 214.

INDEX